THE COOKIEPEDIA

Mixing, Baking, and Reinventing the Classics

By

Stacy Adimando

PHOTOGRAPHS BY
Tara Striano

Library of Congress Cataloging in Publication Number: 2011922698
ISBN: 978-1-59474-535-5

Printed in China
Typeset in Fit Laika, Mavis, Liebe Erika, Merriam
Design and Illustration by Sugar
Art Direction by Katie Hatz
Production management by John J. McGurk
Photographs by Tara Striano
Styling by Penelope Bouklas

Quirk Books
215 Church Street
Philadelphia, PA 19106
quirkbooks.com
10 9 8 7 6 5 4 3 2 1

FOR MY SISTERS,

who know (and may never let me live down) the truth that I wasn't a natural-born baker but ate my experiments anyway. There's no one I'd rather be in the kitchen with. And for my brother, who's always the first in line to taste the results.

"Think what a better world it would be if we all, the whole world, had cookies and milk about three o'clock every afternoon and then lay down on our blankets for a nap."

–ROBERT FULGHUM

TABLE of CONTENTS

HELLO! On a conscious level or not, all bakers know that when their plate of cookies, their tray of chocolate croissants, or their fat slice of five-layer cake hits the table, they will be the most popular person in the room. And that's only half of the fun: It's hard to beat a cozy afternoon in the kitchen, mixing, baking, and reinventing recipes, with the smell of freshly baked cookies wafting through the house.

With that in mind, I filled the pages of this book with recipes that stand to be remembered. It's for the modern home baker who may or may not know all the hows and whys of cookie chemistry just yet, but who gets a rush from learning it—and a little sugar high from the mini-glory that results.

I've always struggled with the concept of having just one career. If I had it my way, I'd turn every passion into a lifetime one and give each hobby the time it deserved to flower into something larger, and longer lasting. Cooking and baking are wonderful in that way. Through simply pursuing my passion for feeding the people I love, I have been a culinary student, a restaurant cook, a magazine writer, a recipe developer, one hell of a hostess (if I may), and now a cookbook author.

As with any creative endeavor—whether it's music, art, or a culinary path—they say you can't truly experiment or reinvent before first mastering the classics. This book gave me the excuse I needed to pay my bakerly dues: months of mixing, testing, and endless cookie eating (not that I'm complaining), inflated gas bills that tallied quickly from 24-hour oven marathons, a permafrost of flour all over my kitchen table and floor, and sore shoulders and feet that I dutifully self-massaged on a nightly basis for the better part of a year. I wouldn't trade a moment of it for the world. First, because it seared into my memory forever the techniques of great cookie baking. And second, because it allowed me to twist and morph and tweak the old-school recipes into something easy and new, and something that is now my own. I'd like to encourage you to do the same: Use this book to bake all the classic cookies our grandmothers used to make and to reinvent them and make them to suit your taste.

I took on this project in full understanding that it'd be tough to improve on the top 50 classic cookie recipes. (But, pssst, we have.) Won't you join me at the oven?

—Stacy

ACKNOWLEDGMENTS

I owe this project, and so much gratitude, to the family, friends, and colleagues who have supported me along this and other culinary journeys. To my mother and father first and always: You are my rocks. Not only have you given me whatever gifts I have, but you endlessly inspire me to use them in new and wonderful ways. To my grandparents Stella, Santa, Frank, and the memory of my grandpa Louie, I am so blessed to have inherited my cooking sense—and many other senses—from you. All my love. To my friends, especially my Brooklyn-based ones, thank you for your patience, faith, and cheerleading. We have so many more kitchen memories to make.

A heartfelt thank-you must go out to my editor Margaret McGuire—an eternal optimist and fellow baker who helped foster this book every step of the way. And to the rest of the team at Quirk as well as Tara Striano, Penelope Bouklas, Jessica O'Brien, and Geraldine Pierson, our wonderful all-lady photo crew. This book is just as much yours as it is mine. Many, many thanks for sharing the experience (and those final batches of cookies) with me.

FInally, to the staff at *Every Day with Rachael Ray*, my chef-instructors at the Institute of Culinary Education, the Savoy kitchen staff, and my dear friends Laura, Kristy, and Rich: You all had a hand in shaping me into the cook I am today. And for that, I am forever indebted.

Now that the sap is out of the way...let's do what we do best.  EAT!

HERE'S the thing about cookies: Unlike most desserts, they actually taste *even better* if they're craggy, homemade, and a little imperfectly shaped. That's why baking cookies is so easy and fun. It's all about spending time with friends and baking together, swapping cookie recipes, and sharing plates of goodies with your neighbors. Roll up your sleeves, make a mess, and have fun!

KITCHEN TOOLS: MEET YOUR NEW BEST FRIENDS

Brownie Pan Brownies made in a glass, nonstick, or dark-colored metal tend to cook a little more quickly and have chewier edges. If you have an insulated metal pan, you may find your brownies need a few extra minutes in the oven. Use the toothpick test to determine doneness.

Cookie Cutters Choose shapes you love. Small details on some cookies may cause the edges to brown more quickly or to break more easily. Keep a close eye on cut cookies in the oven and transfer them carefully after baking.

Cookie Sheets The ideal sheets are thick, heavy, and light-colored metal without major rims. Darker or thinner metals may cause faster browning, but it's not the end of the world. If your sheets are rimmed, flip them over and bake on the unrimmed side for the most even heat distribution.

A slow, gentle rise in temperature is the best way to melt chocolate.

Double Boiler This technically refers to a set of fitted saucepans, but you can create your own double boiler by resting a glass or metal bowl atop a small saucepan. First fill the saucepan with about an inch of water and bring the water to a low simmer. Set the bowl on top—make sure it's *not* touching the water—so the steam can gently heat the bowl, causing a slow rise in temperature. For our purposes, it's primarily used for melting chopped chocolates.

Dry Measuring Cups Spoon dry ingredients like flour, oats, cocoa powder, or sugar lightly into the cup and then level it off by running the straight edge of a knife across the top.

tip

Many baking powder cans have their own built-in edges for leveling.

Food Processor You'll use one for grinding nuts, finely chopping dried fruits, and cutting cold butter into flour to make flaky doughs.

Grater A microplane or the small side of a box grater can be used to zest citrus fruits for flavoring doughs. Move the fruit, not the grater, for the most ease.

Ice Cream or Cookie Scoops Using one of these to spoon out dough onto a cookie sheet provides consistent portions so cookies bake evenly. (They also look purty.)

Liquid Measuring Cups Portioning liquid in one of these means you don't have to fill a dry measuring cup to the top (i.e., risk spilling liquid everywhere), and there's a handy little spout for pouring. Be sure you're measuring with the cup rested on a level surface, and aim for the bottom of the gradation marks as an indicator.

Measuring Spoons For dry ingredients, fill the spoon to the top, then level off with a knife. For liquid ingredients, just fill the spoon up to the tippy top.

Mixing Bowls Baker's rule of thumb: You can never have too many mixing bowls. I keep a few nested sets of stainless ones within reach at all times. Use them for mixing and reserving ingredients, storing egg shells and butter wrappers, and even resting dirty baking tools.

Parchment Paper Lining brownie pans and baking sheets with a piece of this paper treated with a slippery silicone lining usually eliminates the need to grease the pan. *Bonus:* No need to scrub the pan clean after baking! Note that wax paper is not a proper substitute (the waxy coating on it tends to melt under high direct heat).

Piping Bag and Pastry Tips Buying a legit piping bag is worlds above the jury-rigged plastic baggie option, and a dozen or so should cost you only a few bucks. Keep a small and large plain round tip and a small and large star tip handy.

Rolling Pin Handles, no handles, use whatever works for you! If it helps you learn to roll evenly, try sandwiching the chilled dough between two pieces of parchment or wax paper. Peel it away before cutting out cookies.

Sifter There are tools made specifically for this purpose, and if you have them, terrific. Everyone else can use a fine-mesh sieve or strainer.

Small Offset Spatula Because the metal blade is bent where it meets the handle, it provides great control while icing, frosting, or spreading fillings.

Spatula Keep a flexible one handy for scraping down the sides of the mixing bowl and stirring in mix-ins like chocolate chips. (The cook gets dibs on licking it clean.)

Stand Mixer Although you can make most of the cookies in this book without a stand mixer, the recipe steps were in fact written for cooks who have them. Don't fret if you're not one of them. Here are some tips:

- When working with multiple sugars, mash the sugars together first with a fork before adding the butter.
- Act like a mixer. When you're creaming together the butter and sugar, beat hard. Beat well. Use a spatula to firmly press the two together until smooth, fully incorporated, and looking lighter than before (similar to frosting). You shouldn't be able to easily see the sugar granules.

Baker's Best Friend

Wire Rack Meet your new sidekick. A wire baker's rack works wonders for air-cooling cookies quickly and evenly. Because they allow air to circulate around both the top and the bottom of the baked good, they prevent inner moisture from being trapped and sabotaging the nice crisp bottom. They'll save you time and free up your cookie sheet for the next round, too.

COOKIE SPEAK: WHAT WE MEAN WHEN WE SAY...

Baking Ideally, this should happen one cookie sheet at a time in a preheated oven. If you do place two sheets in the oven at once, rotate them halfway through the baking time so they cook as evenly as possible.

Beating Use the paddle attachment on a stand mixer, or use a hand mixer. Start at low speed and work your way up to medium.

Chilling To place dough in the fridge to firm it up, blend, and develop the flavors, let the moisture fully incorporate into the dry ingredients, and let the glutens relax—er, chill. Most cookie doughs will be stiff enough to work with after 30 minutes to an hour in the fridge (or about half that time in the freezer), but the best flavors develop when the dough is left for 2 hours or up to a full day.

TIP: You'll notice darker caramelization and bolder flavors from doughs that have chilled for a longer time.

Cooling This last step determines the cookie's texture. Cookies left to cool on the pan might steam slightly, never fully drying and crisping on the bottom, or continue to bake. For best results, let the cookies set up for a few minutes on the sheet (they'll be less likely to crack and break when you spatula them off), then move them to a wire rack to finish up. Some cookies will deflate slightly as they cool.

TIP: When creaming in a firmer ingredient such as cream cheese, give it a head start in the mixer to bring it to a consistency similar to the butter.

Creaming Beating together butter and sugars to create air pockets (read: a taller, airier cookie). The sugar granules smooth out the fat, leaving behind tiny air holes. To make sure your ingredients really bind together, use room-temperature butter (too cold, it'll be difficult to whip; too melty, and it won't be able to absorb air). Leave it out hours in advance if you can.

Dusting Your instinct is right: This is just fancy baker speak for "sprinkling" (salt or sugar, or spices as it applies in this book). Be generous when you do it, unless otherwise noted. Most cookies expand as they bake, so you need a heavy hand to ensure the flavor reaches right to the edge.

TIP: Let them sit out for a just a few minutes before placing in the oven when ready to bake.

Freezing This can be done to most cookie doughs without damage to the finished product. Either portion the cookies in advance and then freeze them on baking sheets, or freeze the entire ball of dough wrapped twice in plastic wrap and then in aluminum foil.

Greasing Smearing a baking sheet, pan, or piece of parchment with butter to prevent sticking. Greasing may also encourage spreading, so be sure to leave ample room between cookies.

Lining Do yourself—and your cookies—a favor! Layer the cookie sheet with a piece of parchment paper to prevent the treats from sticking to the pan and make cleanup a breeze. If you're baking a ton of cookies, you should be able to reuse the parchment paper (as long as it's not too butter-doused). Just wait a few minutes to ensure it's not retaining heat from the last batch, and use the opposite side the second time around.

Measuring It's important to note that all recipes in this book were made using the spoon-to-cup method of measuring. Use a spoon to transfer the ingredients into the measuring cup (rather than using the cup as a scoop on its own), then level it off with a straight edge, such as the back of a knife Following this technique will produce the best results

Melting Chocolate This might sound like a simple matter of heating, but there is a fascinating science to it. When chocolate melts, the cocoa-butter crystals start to break down and disappear. To keep its stability in the cookie so it holds shape

TIP: Practice your form once or twice before committing to the cookie sheet

without melting at the touch, looks glossy when dry, and "snaps" when you bite into it, it needs to be brought back to temper, a stage where the crystals have reformed. The easiest method: Drop a few chunks of already tempered chocolate of the same kind (the packaged stuff that is still glossy and unblemished) into the melted batch and stir until incorporated. The stable crystals in the chocolate chunks will slowly spread throughout the bowl, making the rest of the chocolate ready to use.

Piping Squeezing dough, icing, or another component through a piping bag to form a decorative pattern. It's best done with a pastry bag and proper pastry tip, but can sometimes be cheated by snipping off the corner of a plastic baggie.

- • To fill a piping bag, cup the area just above the tip in one hand and fold the top half of the bag around your wrist. Use the other hand to fill the bag no more than one-third to one-half of the way with a spatula or spoon, then twist the bag closed and squeeze out the excess air until the batter comes out cleanly.

Rolling Smoothing a dough into an even, thin sheet with a rolling pin and, when noted, a smattering of flour. Channel the Ice Capades when working on a dough. It should have just enough flour beneath it so that it gliiiiiides along the countertop or surface between rolls, gracefully and without sticking. To ensure that's the case, show off its moves—spin it, shift it, and rotate it on the surface after each rolling session.

Scooping Keeping cookies relatively uniform in size will ensure an evenly baked batch. For help getting it right, portion them out with a tool such as a measuring spoon, an ice cream scooper, or a cookie scoop. Take a big dip into the dough, then level off the spoon using the side of the bowl or the straight edge of a butter knife.

Sifting Passing powdery ingredients through a sieve or other perforated tool (I use a fine-mesh colander) rids them of lumps and clumps and aerates them. The result is a lighter cookie and greater ease incorporating the dry ingredients into the wet.

Stirring Do it with a flexible spatula or wooden spoon. Mm-hmm, muscle up.

Testing To test the doneness of brownies, blondies and even some extra-thick cookies, poke the end of a toothpick into the center, and pull out. If there's any gooey batter left on the toothpick, keep baking! Stop when the tester 'pick comes out clean.

TIP: When in doubt, try a taste test.

FUN WITH DECORATING: SHOW OFF YOUR SKILLS WITH THESE COOL TRICKS

Add Texture or Pattern
Pressing one of these kitchen tools into the raw cookies adds instant embellishment.

- a 5-hole citrus zester
- a wire rack
- fork tines
- a meat tenderizer
- a whisk tip
- a kebab skewer

Go nuts with garnishes
Place gorgeous, toasted whole nuts or blanched slivered almonds into the center of cookies just before baking. Brush the area with a little egg white to help them stick. Sprinkles, sanding sugars, nonpareils, and candies are fun, too.

Stick on some stencils
Use an everyday object like a bottle cap as a reverse stencil. Place it in the center of the cookie and sift powdered sugar around the edges.

Pipe a pretty design
Fit a pastry bag with a star tip and fill it with store-bought frosting. Then use it to pipe a pretty star, or a few, onto the top of the cookie.

Doodle
Set cooled cookies on parchment paper or a wire rack with parchment underneath. Dunk a spoon into melted chocolate or a fresh glaze (see simple glaze, page 93, and lemony glaze, page 72), then tip the spoon downward to let some drizzle off. Working with what's left, move the spoon back and forth over the cookies to drizzle manicured stripes or wild designs.

Stick 'em up
Place softer cookies on lollipop or ice-pop sticks to serve to guests in a new way. Or skewer balled cookies on wooden bamboo sticks to make kebab-style cocktail snacks.

Make your mark
Use a rubber stamp to punch words, pictures, or designs into rolled cookies before baking.

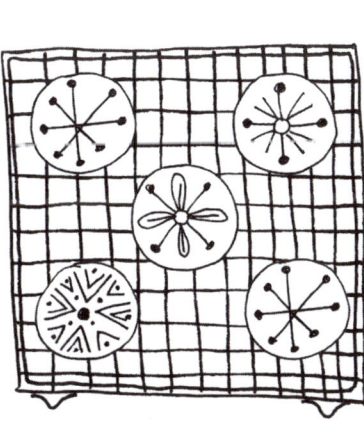

BUTTERY
BUTTERY
NET WT. 4 OZ.
LAND O COOKIES

SHORTBREAD
35

ANIMAL COOKIES
15

CORNMEAL COOKIES
21

SABLES
33

BLONDIES
18

29
ITALIAN BISCUITS

23
EVERYTHING-BUT-THE-
KITCHEN-SINK COOKIES

30
OLD-FASHIONED
SUGAR COOKIES

27
FROSTED
MAPLE PECAN
COOKIES

17
BUTTER BALLS

Animal Cookies
WITH FROSTING AND SPRINKLES

Pulling together this simple dough is practically as easy as opening a box, but it's loads more fun. The dough has a subtle cinnamon flavor, just like the store-bought version.

PREHEAT OVEN TO 350°F

MAKES:
2 DOZEN COOKIES

¾ cup unsalted butter,
    at room temperature

1 cup sugar

1 egg

½ teaspoon vanilla extract

2¼ cups all-purpose flour

1 teaspoon baking powder

½ teaspoon salt

1 teaspoon cinnamon

  Frosting, food dye,
    and decorating sprinkles

 MIX

1. Beat the butter for a minute on its own, then add the sugar a little at a time. Take a break to scrape down the sides of the bowl as needed.

2. Beat in the egg, then the vanilla, until both are fully incorporated. Time for the dry ingredients: Combine the flour, baking powder, salt, and cinnamon and add to the butter mixture half at a time. It might take a while to form a dough. Keep mixing!

3. Turn out the dough onto a clean work surface and shape it into a disk. Chill it for at least 2 hours or overnight.

 BAKE

4. When you're ready to bake, roll out the dough to ⅛-inch thick. Cut out shapes using cookie cutters and place them on parchment-paper-lined sheets 1½ inches apart. If the dough is soft, stick the sheets in the freezer

 tip

If it's tricky to roll your dough at first, just let it hang out at room temperature for a few minutes to soften slightly.

 CONTINUED

Animal Cookies, cont'd...

for 15 minutes (or in the fridge for 30). Then bake the cookies until golden, 10 to 12 minutes. Frost when completely cooled.

ADD A SPLASH OF COLOR

Swirly tie-dye cookie dough is fun to make, especially for animal cookies.

Tie-Dye Animals

Divide the dough in half before chilling. Add a few drops red or blue food coloring to one half and knead the dough to incorporate. Add a few drops green or blue food coloring to the other half and incorporate. Recombine the doughs, pressing your fingers through them just enough so the colors start to blend together, but don't fully mix. Chill, roll, cut, and bake your tie-dyed creations.

NOTES:

Butter Balls

Even though holiday meals with my family are so huge we rarely have room for dessert, it wouldn't be Christmas without Grandma Stella's butter balls. I'm convinced years of rolling meatballs has helped her perfect the technique—you can't dawdle or the butter gets melty between your fingers. Full or not, everyone in your family will toss back a few. Thanks, Grandma.

PREHEAT OVEN TO 350°F

MAKES:
2½ DOZEN COOKIES

1	cup unsalted butter, at room temperature
½	cup powdered sugar, plus more for rolling
1¼	teaspoon vanilla extract
2	cups all-purpose flour
¾	teaspoon salt
1½	cups chopped walnuts

 MIX

1. Cream together the butter and powdered sugar until light and fluffy. Mix in the vanilla. Add the flour and salt and continue mixing until a dough forms. Gently stir in walnuts by hand.

 BAKE

2. Chill dough in the fridge until firm, about 1 hour. Roll it into 1-inch balls, then place them on cookie sheets 2 inches apart. Bake until just set but not yet browning, about 10 to 12 minutes.

MORE TO TRY

Chocolate Butter Balls
Add 2 teaspoons cocoa powder to the flour before mixing it in.

Pecan Butter Balls
Substitute chopped toasted pecans for the walnuts.

NOTES:

Blondies
WITH BROWN BUTTER

These bigger, nuttier bar versions of chocolate chip cookies get their distinct flavor from browned butter, and they have a denser, satisfying chew. A sprinkling of coarse salt on the tops brings out a rich flavor.

PREHEAT OVEN TO 350°F

MAKES: 2 DOZEN BARS

1 cup unsalted butter
2 cups all-purpose flour
1 teaspoon baking powder
1 teaspoon salt
1½ cups light brown sugar
½ cup sugar
2 eggs
1½ teaspoons vanilla extract
⅔ cup chocolate chips
⅔ cup toasted pecans, chopped
Coarse salt such as sea or kosher, for sprinkling (optional)

 MIX

1. Start by browning the butter. Melt it in a saucepan on medium heat. When the foaming subsides, start swirling the pan to keep the butter moving. Continue to cook until it changes from a light yellow to a deep golden, stopping just when you see the color change happen. Take it off the heat and pour into a bowl to cool.

2. Meanwhile, sift the flour, baking powder, and salt into a bowl and set aside.

3. Beat the melted butter and sugars together. Add the eggs and vanilla and beat for several minutes, or until the mixture looks thick and silky. Add the dry ingredients one-third at a time and mix until combined. Stir in the chocolate chips and pecans.

 tip

If you take it too far, a matter of about 30 seconds to a minute, the butter will burn.

4. Grease a 9-by-13-inch baking pan. Line the bottom of the pan with parchment paper, then grease the parchment paper.

5. Pour the dough onto the parchment paper and spread it evenly with a spatula or slightly wet hand. Bake 30 to 35 minutes (err on the shorter side for doughier blondies), until a toothpick inserted in the center comes out clean.

6. Sprinkle lightly with the coarse salt. Let cool completely before removing from the pan. Cut into squares.

tip

Lift using the two long sides of the parchment paper, or turn it out onto a cutting board.

MAKE 'EM YOUR WAY

Just like chocolate chip cookie dough, blondie batter is great for sneaking in extra treats and adjusting the amount of mix-ins to suit your personal taste. Some people prefer just a few semisweet chocolate chips, others like to load their blondies chock full of goodies.

Candy Bar Blondies
Mix in roughly chopped candy bars, or roughly chopped dark chocolate.

Platinum Blondies
Use white chocolate chips and macadamia nuts.

NOTES:

Cornmeal Cookies
WITH ROSEMARY

These crumbly, sweet, and savory bites make a beautiful drop-by offering tied with baker's twine and packed into gift boxes or goodie bags. And they're a treat to bake, because when they're about halfway done, you'll smell the pungent rosemary aroma seeping out of your oven.

PREHEAT OVEN TO 350°F

MAKES: 2 DOZEN COOKIES

¾   cup salted butter,
        at room temperature
½   cup sugar
2   egg yolks
1   teaspoon vanilla extract
1¼ cups all-purpose flour
½   cup cornmeal
1   teaspoon baking powder
¼   teaspoon salt
    Dried rosemary (optional)

 MIX

1. Cream the butter and sugar until fluffy. Add the egg yolks and beat well. Mix in the vanilla.

2. Stir together the flour, cornmeal, baking powder, and salt. Add them a third at a time to the butter mixture and beat until incorporated. Form the dough into a ball, wrap it tightly in plastic wrap, and stick it in the fridge until firm, about 1 hour.

 BAKE

3. Roll out dough on a lightly floured board to ¼-inch thick. Cut out cookies using a 2½-inch cutter and place them an inch apart on a lightly greased cookie sheet. Sprinkle each top with a few pieces of rosemary, lightly pressing the herb to adhere.

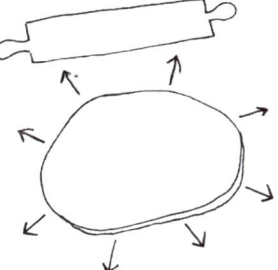

 CONTINUED

Cornmeal Cookies, cont'd...

4. Bake until the edges start to turn golden,
10 to 12 minutes.

ADD A CITRUS TWIST

These crumbly golden cookies are delicious
with citrusy flavors.

Orangey
*Add the grated zest of 1 orange into the butter
while mixing. The rosemary garnish is optional.*

Lemony
*Add the grated zest of $\frac{1}{2}$ lemon into the butter
while mixing.*

Limey
*Add the grated zest of $\frac{1}{2}$ lime into the butter
while mixing, and skip the rosemary garnish.*

NOTES:

Everything-but-the-Kitchen-Sink Cookies

If cookies could talk, I'm sure they'd tell us loud and clear that they're not just partial to sweet mix-ins like chocolate chips—salty treats are yummy, too! So, yes, those are corn chips and pretzels sharing a cookie with sweet coconut and peanut butter chips. Now, if the thought of a crunchy, salty bite blended in to this soft, sugary dough doesn't speak to you, well, you have some thinking to do.

PREHEAT OVEN TO 375°F

MAKES:
1½ DOZEN COOKIES

1   cup unsalted butter,
     at room temperature

1   cup sugar

½   cup packed light-brown sugar

2   teaspoons vanilla extract

1   egg, plus 1 egg white

2   cups all-purpose flour

1   teaspoon baking soda

1   teaspoon baking powder

1   teaspoons kosher salt

1   cup of your favorite sweet
     add-ins*

1½ cups of your favorite
     salty snacks**

   ✱ I like peanut butter
     chips, sweetened
     coconut flakes, and
     dark chocolate chips.

  ✱✱ I use Fritos, potato
     chips, and pretzels.

MIX

1. Line 2 large baking sheets with parchment paper and set them aside. Cream the butter and both sugars on medium speed for a few minutes, until they look light and fluffy. Add the vanilla and eggs and continue to beat on low speed until well combined, scraping down the sides of the bowl as needed.

2. In the meantime, whisk together the flour, baking soda, baking powder, and salt. Add the dry ingredients to the wet mixture in two batches, beating slowly after each addition, until fully incorporated.

3. Pour your sweet mix-ins into the bowl. Break up the salty snacks into smaller cookie-friendly pieces and dump those in as well. Use a spatula to stir them together. It should look like a ton of mix-ins. That's good.

CONTINUED

Everything-but-the-Kitchen-Sink Cookies, cont'd...

BAKE

4. Portion 2 heaping tablespoons of dough at a time into imperfect balls and place them at least 2 inches apart on the lined baking sheets. Bake, rotating sheets halfway through, until cookies are golden brown, about 16 to 18 minutes. Transfer to a wire rack to cool.

THROW IN THE KITCHEN SINK

Here's a list of tasty mix-ins you can stir into the cookie dough. Mix and match your favorite snacks!

- Honey-roasted nuts
- Whole espresso beans
- Sprinkles
- White chocolate chips
- Tortilla chips
- Cheese puffs
- Toffee bits
- Maple candies
- Yogurt raisins
- Asian snack mix
- Wasabi peas
- Chocolate shavings
- Breakfast cereal
- Cool Ranch Doritos*
- Granola
- Salted corn nuts
- Chocolate-covered peanuts

✱ A personal favorite! Don't judge.

NOTES:

Frosted Maple Pecan Cookies

One Sunday morning, leave your pancake batter in the pantry and bake a batch of these instead. Pure maple syrup sweetens the cookie dough and gives it a lovely rich aroma. Bonus: lots of frosting.

PREHEAT OVEN TO 350°F

MAKES: 2 DOZEN COOKIES

1½ cups all-purpose flour
1½ teaspoon baking soda
¼ teaspoon salt
½ cup unsalted butter,
      at room temperature
½ cup sugar
1 egg
1½ teaspoons vanilla extract
¾ cup pure maple syrup
1 cup chopped pecans
    Homemade frosting
      (page 28)

MIX

1. Toast the nuts in a 350°F oven until just starting to turn golden and smell nutty, about 10 minutes. Set aside to cool.

2. Sift together the flour, baking soda, and salt into a bowl and set it aside.

3. Cream together the butter and sugar until the mixture looks light and fluffy. Then add the egg and vanilla and mix these in until combined.

4. Pour in the maple syrup and mix that in as well as you can.

5. Add the reserved flour mixture and nuts; beat until just combined. Turn out the dough onto a piece of plastic wrap, cover, and chill for about 30 minutes to an hour, until firm.

BAKE 6. Drop tablespoon-sized balls of dough onto the cookie sheets about 2½ inches apart

tip

Chilling the dough makes for tall, chewy cookies.

CONTINUED

Frosted Maple Pecan Cookies, cont'd...

They'll be a light golden when they're done.

(they'll spread a fair amount). Flatten them slightly with the palm of your hand. Bake 10 to 12 minutes and whip up some frosting while you're waiting. Cool completely before slathering on the frosting.

HOMEMADE FROSTING

Maple pecan cookies are delicious even if you skip the topping. But why would you go and do that?!

Creamy Vanilla Frosting

Combine 1 cup powdered sugar, 1/4 cup heavy cream, and 1 teaspoon pure vanilla extract. Beat until smooth and creamy.

NOTES:

Italian Biscuits

Growing up, we'd refer to these as S cookies in my family. We kids never ate them ("You mean they're just plain??"), and they were always store-bought rather than freshly made. Slowly but surely our dad would finish out the package over a series of morning cups of tea. Not only are they simple, they keep for weeks, fill you up, and perfectly soak up a warm drink. Now when I bake them in my own house, I'm responsible for finishing the batch. Sometimes it's so hard being a grownup.

PREHEAT OVEN TO 350°F

MAKES:
2 DOZEN COOKIES

4	tablespoons unsalted butter
1¾	cups plus 2 tablespoons all-purpose flour
1½	teaspoons baking powder
¼	teaspoon salt
2	eggs
⅓	cup sugar
1½	teaspoons vanilla extract

MIX

1. Melt the butter and set aside to cool slightly. Sift the flour, baking powder, and salt into a bowl and set it aside.

2. With a mixer, beat the eggs on medium speed for a minute. Add the sugar in a slow, steady stream, continuing to mix on medium until they're combined. Reduce the speed to low and slowly add the cooled butter and vanilla.

3. Add the flour mixture and mix on low speed just until the dough comes together.

BAKE

4. Scoop out tablespoon-sized balls of dough and roll them between your fingers into ropes about 5 inches long. Gently form the ropes into S shapes. Place the cookies on sheets about 2 inches from one another. Let them sit for 15 minutes before baking.

5. Bake cookies for 15 to 18 minutes, until they're golden brown and delicious.

tip

Resting the dough will help the cookies plump up when they're in the oven.

Old-Fashioned Sugar Cookies
WITH VANILLA SUGAR

This is one of those recipes you can make just once and *almost* remember by heart the next time. The dough is so simple, and comes together so easily, it's a real confidence-booster. This version makes a softer, fluffier cookie—not the firmer type you might see decorated around the holidays—and they sparkle from a generous dusting of vanilla sugar or turbinado sugar instead of colored frosting. I think they taste even better the second day.

PREHEAT OVEN TO 325°F

MAKES:
2 DOZEN COOKIES

3 cups all-purpose flour

1 teaspoon baking soda

½ teaspoon kosher salt

1 cup unsalted butter,
      at room temperature

1¾ cups sugar

¼ cup light brown sugar

2 eggs, beaten

2 teaspoons vanilla extract
      Vanilla sugar* (or turbinado),
      for dusting

✳ To make your own, push 1 fresh vanilla bean into 4 cups of sugar in an airtight container. Let sit for a week before using.

MIX

1. Sift the flour, baking soda, and salt into a big bowl and whisk them together gently. Set the bowl aside.

2. Cream the butter and sugars for several minutes, until they look light and fluffy. Add the eggs and vanilla and mix just until combined. Reduce the speed and add the flour mixture into the butter mixture little by little, about a third at a time. Mix until no more white flour is showing, stopping to scrape down the sides of the bowl if needed.

3. Cover the dough in plastic wrap and stick it in the freezer or fridge until chilled and firm. About 20 minutes in the freezer or 45 minutes in the fridge should do it.

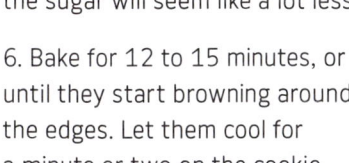

4. Remove the dough, break off pieces, and roll them quickly into 1-inch balls. (Try not to dawdle over it—the goal is to keep the dough chilly.) Place them on parchment-paper-lined cookie sheets about 2 inches apart from one another, then use the palm of your hand to slightly flatten and even out the balls. (For dome-shaped cookies, flatten less. For thinner cookies, flatten more.)

5. Sprinkle with the vanilla sugar. Use more than you think you want—when the cookies spread, the sugar will seem like a lot less.

6. Bake for 12 to 15 minutes, or until they start browning around the edges. Let them cool for a minute or two on the cookie sheet before lifting them to a rack to cool.

tip

To help granulated or vanilla sugar adhere, try lightly wetting the tops of the flattened cookies with your fingers before sprinkling it on.

tip

You can roll the dough and cut out shapes instead.

ADD A TWIST

If you like citrus, try this variation of the standard cookie recipe.

Sweet Grapefruit Sugar Cookies

Add to the dough before chilling: 1 tablespoon plus 1 teaspoon grapefruit juice, 2 teaspoons finely grated grapefruit zest (try to avoid the white pith). After baking, when they've cooled enough to firm up, toss them in powdered sugar.

NOTES:

Sables
WITH LEMON ZEST

Of course these enviable treats are French. (And in France, you'll see them written as *sablés*, pronounced *sah-blays*.) They're petite but substantial and not too sweet. Nibble off the sugary edges first, then dunk the remaining lemony center in a cup of coffee or milky tea.

PREHEAT OVEN TO 350°F

MAKES:
2½ DOZEN COOKIES

1 cup unsalted butter, at room temperature

¾ cup sugar

½ teaspoon salt

Scant ½ teaspoon lemon zest

2 egg yolks, at room temperature*

2 cups all-purpose flour

¼ cup coarse sugar or sanding sugar, for decorating

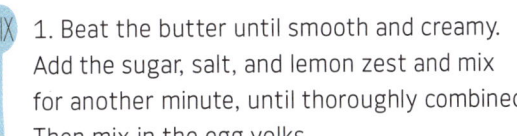 MIX 1. Beat the butter until smooth and creamy. Add the sugar, salt, and lemon zest and mix for another minute, until thoroughly combined. Then mix in the egg yolks.

2. Gradually add the flour and beat until the dough looks moist. Divide the dough in half and roll each half into an 8-inch log. Wrap logs in parchment paper and refrigerate overnight.

BAKE 3. When you're ready to bake, grease a few cookie sheets or line them with parchment paper. Pull out the dough and brush the egg white over the outside. Sprinkle the sanding sugar all over the log, rolling it around a bit to be sure the sugar sticks.

4. Using a sharp knife, cut the log into ¼-inch-thick slices and place them on cookie sheets about 1 inch apart.

tip

For perfectly light and crumbly sables, chill logs of dough overnight or up to 3 days before baking.

＊ Save the whites in the fridge if baking the same day. Brushed onto cookies before baking, they help crystals of sanding sugar stick onto the dough.

CONTINUED

Sables, cont'd...

5. Bake for 12 to 15 minutes, until the cookies are browned around the edges.

MORE TO TRY

This classic cookie recipe is fun to play around with.

Holiday Sables
Alternate rolling the cookies in green and red decorating sprinkles instead of turbinado sugar.

Nutty Sables
Roll the sables in finely crushed toasted pecans instead of sugar.

NOTES:

YUMMY

Shortbread
IN WEDGES, ROUNDS, OR BARS

Although the sprinkled, studded, and frosted cookies might win the popularity contest on an assorted tray, shortbread is truly the king of cookies and will always have its die-hard fans. Anyone who can perfect this cookie is a baker in my book, not because it's especially difficult, but because it's the ultimate classic—confident in all its refined, crumbly, buttery glory. This cookie is anything but plain.

PREHEAT OVEN TO 325°F

MAKES:
3 DOZEN COOKIES

1½ cups all-purpose flour

½ cup rice flour*

1 cup unsalted butter,
      at room temperature

½ cup sugar

¼ teaspoon salt

¾ teaspoon vanilla extract

* If you can't find rice flour, just use all-purpose flour instead.

MIX

1. Whisk both flours together in a bowl and set aside.

2. Cream together the butter, sugar, salt, and vanilla on medium speed for a few minutes until light and fluffy. Remove the bowl from the mixer and stir in the flours by hand with a wooden spoon.

3. Turn out the dough onto a clean surface. Working quickly, use the heat of your hands to make a solid ball. Pull out a large piece of plastic wrap, and flatten the dough on top of it into a ¾-inch-thick rectangle.

4. Double wrap it and refrigerate for 2 hours (and up to 2 weeks) to firm.

tip

It's nice to have shortbread dough in the fridge to bake off on a rainy day.

CONTINUED

Shortbread, cont'd...

 5. Grease several cookie sheets with butter or line them with parchment paper. Place the dough on a lightly floured surface and dust the top of it and your rolling pin with a little flour, too. Gently roll it to ¼-inch thick for thin cookies or ¾-inch thick for bars.

6. Using a knife or pizza cutter, cut the dough into 2-inch-by-1-inch rectangles. (Or cut out cookies into circles or wedges.) Place the cookies on sheets about 1 inch apart. Prick the centers with a fork.

7. Bake for 15 to 17 minutes (add an additional 2 to 3 minutes for thicker bars), until the edges are lightly golden. Cool sheets on wire racks.

Psst: Treat the fork pricks like decorations— you will see them in the finished result.

VARIATIONS

Shortbread dough is easy to adapt: Try adding flavors like the ones below or experiment with cookie cutters to make different shapes.

Espresso Shortbread
Add 2 teaspoons instant espresso powder to the flours before mixing. Dip one end in melted chocolate. (Follow the dipping directions for the Poppy Seed Squares on page 146.)

Lavender-Lemon Shortbread
Beat 1 teaspoon dried chopped culinary lavender and 1/2 teaspoon lemon zest into the butter and sugar mixture in step 2.

NOTES:

MORE SHORTBREAD SHAPES TO TRY

Wedges
Press the dough into a circular glass or metal pan lined with parchment paper. Slice like a pizza before cooking.

Coins
Roll the dough to $1/4$-inch and use a small cookie or biscuit cutter.

Diamonds
Press dough into a square glass or metal pan lined with parchment paper. Before baking, slice dough diagonally into 2-inch strips. Then slice from top to bottom to form diamond shapes.

Shards
Roll out the dough but do not cut it into cookies before baking. When cooled, break the cookie into rustic pieces with your hands.

Dominos
Using a sharp knife, cut the raw dough into $1 1/2$-inch squares. Then use a skewer to poke 4 holes in the center.

NOTES:

CHOCOLATY

CHOCOLATE + COOKIES = AWESOMENESS

45
CRINKLES

43
CHOCOLATE CHIP COOKIES

49
CHOCOLATE SANDWICH COOKIES

55
MINT THINS

40
BROWNIES

51
CHOCOLATE
SPRITZ
COOKIES

58
TRIPLE
CHOCOLATE
COOKIES

53
FLORENTINES

Brownies

It's hard to imagine a time when brownies wouldn't be a hit, but there's something particularly special about them when they're homemade. Owed in part to a not-shy helping of good baking cocoa, this version has the most satisfying chew, somewhere between a thick cookie and a piece of fudgy chocolate cake. They take a little longer than most cookies to bake, but the batter is almost unbotchable. And, hello, are they not worth the wait?

PREHEAT OVEN TO 350°F

MAKES: 1⅓ DOZEN COOKIES

¾ cup unsalted butter
1 cup all-purpose flour
½ cup cocoa powder
¾ teaspoon baking powder
½ teaspoon salt
1¼ cups sugar
3 eggs
1½ teaspoons vanilla extract

MIX
1. Heat the butter until it's just melted and set it aside. In the meantime, combine the flour, cocoa powder, baking powder, and salt in a bowl and set aside.

2. Pour the butter into the sugar and beat until the mixture looks smooth and thick. Add the eggs, one at a time, beating each until incorporated. Then add the vanilla.

3. Start adding in the flour mixture about a third at a time, beating after each addition to let the dry ingredients incorporate. When it starts to look like brownie batter, you're done.

BAKE
4. Grease a 9-inch square glass or metal baking pan and pour in the batter. Bake for 25 to 30 minutes, until a toothpick inserted in the center of the brownies comes out clean. Let cool completely before cutting.

tip

For easier removal you can layer a piece of parchment on top of the greased pan, and grease the paper, too.

VARIATION

White chocolate gets a bad rap. But when it's melted into rich chocolaty brownies like these, even the biggest naysayers will fall in love.

White Chocolate Chip Brownies

Sprinkle 1½ cups white chocolate chips into the finished batter. Reserve the last handful for sprinkling on top just before baking.

NOTES:

Chocolate Chip Cookies
WITH BITTERSWEET CHIPS

Everyone has a different opinion about what makes the perfect chocolate chip cookie. None of us are wrong! You can transform it from soft to chewy and chunky to crisp with a few simple variations. This version has a deeper, molasses flavor and a softer texture thanks to the addition of brown sugar. Watching a few plump up through the oven window is an unbeatable way to spend a Sunday afternoon.

PREHEAT OVEN TO 350°F

MAKES: 2 DOZEN COOKIES

1⅓ cups all-purpose flour

½ teaspoon baking soda

½ teaspoon kosher salt

½ cup unsalted butter, at room temperature

⅓ cup sugar

½ cup light brown sugar

1 large egg

¾ teaspoon vanilla extract

1 cup (about 8 oz) bittersweet chocolate chips or chunks*

 MIX

1. Sift the flour, baking soda, and salt into a big bowl and stir. Set the bowl aside.

2. Cream the butter and sugars for several minutes, until they look light and fluffy. Add the egg and vanilla extract and mix until just combined. Add the flour mixture right into the butter mixture. Mix on low speed until they're incorporated. Then the fun part: Stir in the chocolate chips.

 BAKE

3. Go down the line dropping tablespoon-sized balls of dough onto parchment-paper-lined cookie sheets. Leave about 2 inches between them so they have plenty of room to spread. Bake for 8 to 10 minutes, rotating the sheets halfway through baking.

tip

For the thickest, chewiest cookies, chill the dough for 1 to 2 hours—or overnight—before baking.

✳ Some supermarket brands of chips are made to resist melting. So if you like an ooey, gooey, melty cookie, opt for chunks.

CONTINUED

Chocolate Chip Cookies, cont'd...

4. Try one hot out of the oven, but let the rest cool for a minute or two before lifting them to a rack to cool. If you get melted chocolate on your hands, you're eating these too slowly.

MORE TO TRY

The variations are endless. Here are a few of my favorites.

Chocolate Chip Cookies with Peanut Brittle and Sea Salt
Add 4 ounces crushed peanut brittle to the dough when you mix in the chocolate chips. Sprinkle the formed cookies lightly with sea salt just before baking.

Double Chocolate Chips with Pistachios
Replace the chips with half dark chocolate and half white chocolate chips, and mix a few handfuls of shelled unsalted pistachios.

Extra Chocolaty Chocolate Chips
Grate a few ounces of semisweet chocolate directly into the batter, and increase the chips by 1/2 cup.

NOTES:

Crinkles
WITH POWDERED SUGAR

Bake these craggy little puffs any day. They're fancy enough for dinner parties, holidays, or special occasions, but they have a down-home fudgy flavor and—with a poof of powdered sugar—aren't meant to look perfect. Speaking of which, don't skimp on the powdered sugar: It's the secret to their gorgeous cracked tops.

PREHEAT OVEN TO 325°F

MAKES:
4 DOZEN COOKIES*

*But they're little!

6 oz bittersweet chocolate, finely chopped

¼ cup plus 2 tablespoons unsalted butter, at room temperature

½ cup sugar

2 eggs

1 teaspoon vanilla extract

1½ cups all-purpose flour

2 tablespoons cocoa powder

¾ teaspoon baking powder

¼ teaspoon salt

Powdered sugar for rolling

MIX

1. Set a small pot of water on the stove and bring it to a simmer. Place the chopped chocolate and the butter into a glass or metal bowl and set the bowl over the simmering water. (Be sure the bottom of the bowl does not touch the water. It's the heat from the steam that we want here.) Let the chocolate start to melt, then stir occasionally until it's smooth. Remove from the heat and set aside.

2. Beat the sugar and eggs on medium speed for several minutes, until they're thick and smooth. Add the vanilla extract and melted chocolate and keep on beating on medium-low speed until they're combined.

3. Sift the flour, cocoa powder, baking powder, and salt into a separate bowl. Add the mixture in two batches, beating each time until just

CONTINUED

Crinkles, cont'd...

combined. Cover the dough with plastic wrap and let it chill in the refrigerator for about 2 hours, or until firm enough to scoop.

BAKE 4. Line a few cookie sheets with parchment paper or silicone mats. Roll 1-inch balls of dough with your fingers, then toss them around in a bowl of powdered sugar, coating them completely. Place them about 1½ inches apart on the cookie sheets. Bake for 8 to 10 minutes, rotating the sheets halfway through baking, until they just start to feel firm. Cool the sheets for 5 minutes before transferring the cookies to the wire racks to finish cooling.

tip

These are best when slightly undercooked in the center.

VARIATIONS

Add a Shot of Espresso
Calling all coffee lovers! Add 1 teaspoon instant espresso powder into the melted chocolate just before removing from heat.

Candy Cane Crinkles
Mix finely crushed candy cane pieces into the dough before chilling.

NOTES:

Chocolate Sandwich Cookies
WITH CREAM FILLING

I had a fantasy of baking homemade sandwich cookies that taste just like the store-bought kind I ate as a kid. But when they turned out tasting like a grown-up version—rich cocoa, a more delicate crisp, and a vanilla-bean-tinged cream—I had no complaints. A little burst of salt in the dough is the perfect contrast to the sweet filling. These treats taste best the second day, when the icing has had a chance to settle into its new cookie home.

PREHEAT OVEN TO 350°F

MAKES: 1½ DOZEN COOKIES

½ cup sugar

¼ cup light brown sugar

1½ cups all-purpose flour

¾ cup cocoa powder

½ teaspoon baking soda

1 teaspoon salt

¾ cup unsalted butter, cut into small pieces, at room temperature

1 large egg

1 teaspoon vanilla extract

Cream Filling:

⅓ cup unsalted butter, at room temperature

1 teaspoon vanilla extract

¼ teaspoon salt

1½ cups powdered sugar

1 to 2 tablespoons whole milk or half-and-half

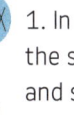 MIX

1. In a mixer or food processor, mix together the sugars, flour, cocoa powder, baking soda, and salt on low speed. With the motor running, add the butter a few pieces at a time and pulse to incorporate. Add the egg and vanilla and continue pulsing until the dough starts to form.

2. Turn out the dough onto a clean surface and form it into a disk. Chill at least 1 hour, or overnight, until firm.

 BAKE

3. When you're ready to bake, cut the dough in half and roll out each piece to about ⅛-inch thick. Cut out small 1- to 2-inch rounds and place them on parchment-paper-lined baking sheets about 1 inch apart. Bake for 12 to 15 minutes or until dry.

 tip

When cutting out cookie shapes, only reroll the dough scraps once. Any more than that will toughen the dough.

CONTINUED

4. Set the sheets on wire racks for about 5 minutes before transferring cookies directly onto racks to cool.

5. While the cookies cool, make the filling. In a mixer, beat together the butter, vanilla, and salt until they look light and fluffy. Add the powdered sugar slowly, with your mixer on low speed. Beat until fully incorporated. Add the milk one tablespoon at a time and beat until the filling is at a spreadable consistency.

tip

Err on the side of too thick here. I find it easier to tell when I work the mixture with a spatula by hand for the last few moments of mixing.

6. Spoon, spread, or pipe a small dollop of filling onto the center of half the cookies. Top with another cookie, pressing until the filling spreads to the edges.

CREAMY COOKIE FILLINGS

Try these flavors or invent your own. Double the filling recipes for double-stuffed cookies.

Peanut Butter Sandwich Filling

Mash together 3 tablespoons unsalted butter (at room temperature), $^3/_4$ cup peanut butter, $^2/_3$ cup confectioners' sugar, and $^1/_4$ teaspoon salt.

Peppermint Cream Filling

Add $^1/_4$ to $^1/_2$ teaspoon pure peppermint extract (depending on how strong you like it) to the cream filling.

NOTES:

Chocolate Spritz Cookies

If you don't have a cookie press, you can shape these cookies any way you like using a star-tipped piping bag. See pages 8–9 for an explainer.

PREHEAT OVEN TO 375°F

MAKES: 4 DOZEN COOKIES

½ cup vegetable shortening

½ cup butter

¾ cup sugar

1 egg

2 teaspoons vanilla extract

2¼ cups all-purpose flour

¼ cup plus 2 tablespoons cocoa

¼ teaspoon baking powder

¼ teaspoon salt

Colored sugars or nonpareils, for decorating

 MIX

1. Cream together the shortening and butter until smooth. Stream in the sugar gradually while beating, continuing to beat until it looks light and fluffy.

2. Sift the flour, cocoa, baking powder, and salt together and set them aside.

3. Add the egg and vanilla and beat well.

4. Add the flour mixture, a third at a time, mixing until all batches are well incorporated. Turn out the dough onto a piece of parchment paper and chill it until it sets up slightly, 20 to 30 minutes.

 BAKE

5. Load the dough into either a cookie press or a pastry bag fitted with star tip; pipe them out, about 2 inches apart from one another,

CONTINUED

Chocolate Spritz Cookies, cont'd...

on ungreased cookie sheets. Decorate them with sprinkles or sugars and bake for 7 to 8 minutes, until the cookies look set up. Let cool slightly before transferring.

MAKE THEM YOUR WAY

Spritz cookies were made for the holidays, so it's fun to experiment with colorful doughs and festive decorations.

Holiday Spritz
Leave out the chocolate and add 3 or 4 drops of red, green, or other food coloring. Decorate with sprinkles, nonpareils, or big red cinnamon candies.

NOTES:

Florentines
WITH CHOCOLATE DRIZZLES

My dad's family is from Italy; my mom's family is from Italy. And yet I never saw either side bake a fresh Florentine. So I will happily start the tradition! With all the melting, shaping, and drizzling, it's a fun artsy endeavor, and the result is exquisite. This is one cookie that tastes best immediately after cooling, so you have to pawn them off quickly. I don't think anyone will mind.

PREHEAT OVEN TO 375°F

MAKES:
3 DOZEN COOKIES

1	cup unsalted butter, at room temperature
1¼	cups sugar
2	tablespoons corn syrup
1	tablespoon all-purpose flour
⅓	cup heavy cream
¼	teaspoon salt
2⅓	cups sliced almonds
4	ounces roughly chopped bittersweet chocolate

MIX

1. Line a few cookie sheets with parchment paper or silicone baking mats. Set them aside.

2. Melt the butter, sugar, and corn syrup together over medium heat. Add the flour and whisk to combine. Add the cream and salt and do the same.

3. Let cook until the mixture comes to a full boil, then add in the almonds and stir to combine. Continue cooking for 3 more minutes, until the mixture thickens and starts to move around the pan as one mass. Take the pan off the heat.

BAKE

4. Drop 4 small spoonfuls of dough onto cookie sheets, leaving as much room between them as possible (the baked cookies will spread to about triple the size).

 CONTINUED

Florentines, cont'd...

5. Using an offset spatula or a wet hand, spread and flatten the batter into 3-inch rounds, creating a thin layer.

6. Bake for 5 to 8 minutes, or until edges are brown and centers are just turning golden.

tip

If they harden too fast, just return them to the oven for a minute or so.

7. Remove the cookie sheets from the oven and immediately reshape the cookies back into 3-inch circles, using the offset spatula or the back of a spoon to drag the batter back into place and round out the edges. The cookies will harden within a few minutes.

8. Cool the reshaped cookies on sheets until they are firm and cool enough to handle. Then move them to a wire rack covered in parchment paper to set completely.

9. As the optional (though delicious and suggested) finisher, melt the chocolate, in a glass or metal bowl over a pot of simmering water on the stove. Drizzle the melted chocolate over the tops of the Florentines. Let harden.

ADD ICE CREAM

These sweet and thin cookies are perfect for making ice-cream sandwich cookies in the summertime.

Florentine Ice Cream Sandwiches
When the cookies have cooled completely, skip the chocolate drizzle. Let a container of coffee or vanilla ice cream sit out, or microwave it at 10-second intervals, until it's soft enough to dollop. In the meantime, lay half the Florentines on a parchment-lined baking sheet flat side up. Drop a heaping spoonful of the softened ice cream (about 2 to 3 tablespoons) into the center of each. Top with the remaining cookies and press lightly to adhere. Cover the baking sheet loosely with foil and place in the freezer at least 2 hours.

NOTES:

Mint Thins

Nobody you know will *not* come by when you say you're baking homemade mint thins. (If they don't so much as ask, consider defriending them immediately.) The question is: Do you want to share? The baking and dunking takes no time (especially if you're tasting as you go), but these bite-size treats do hold up best (and taste yummiest) once the mint chocolate has had ample time to set. If you're protective of your stash, store them in the freezer. They're best with a chill anyway.

PREHEAT OVEN TO 350°F

MAKES: 3½ DOZEN COOKIES

1 cup unsalted butter, at room temperature

1 cup powdered sugar

1 egg

1 teaspoon vanilla extract

1½ cups all-purpose flour

⅔ cup cocoa powder

¼ teaspoon salt

12 ounces semisweet chocolate

¼ cup unsalted butter

¾ teaspoon peppermint flavor

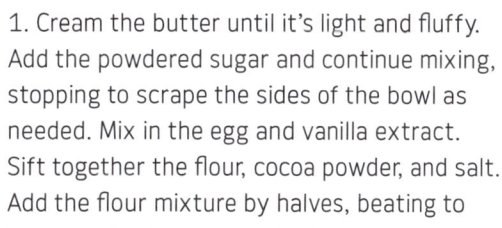

MIX

1. Cream the butter until it's light and fluffy. Add the powdered sugar and continue mixing, stopping to scrape the sides of the bowl as needed. Mix in the egg and vanilla extract. Sift together the flour, cocoa powder, and salt. Add the flour mixture by halves, beating to incorporate after each addition.

2. Turn out the dough onto a clean surface and form it into a disk with your hands. Split the disk in half and place them in the fridge to firm up for 1 hour.

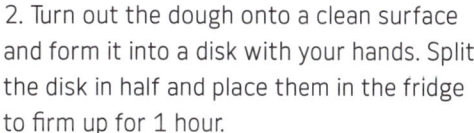

BAKE

3. Working on a floured surface (you'll need a decent amount, since the dough is sticky), roll out the dough to ⅛-inch thick. Shape the cookies using a 1½-inch round cutter and place them on a parchment-paper-lined baking

tip

If you're short on time, do 25 minutes in the freezer instead.

CONTINUED

Mint Thins, cont'd...

sheet. Bake for 10 to 12 minutes, then let cool completely.

4. Break up the chocolate into a bowl and set it over a small pot of simmering water (make sure the bowl doesn't touch the water). Add the butter and the peppermint flavor and stir the mixture steadily until it's fully melted and looks glossy and smooth. Remove the bowl and let the chocolate cool slightly.

5. One by one, drop the cookies in the chocolate, then scoop them out with a fork to let the excess drip off. (Tap the cookies against the side of the bowl to help drain the extra chocolate.) Move them carefully to a wire rack or parchment-paper-lined baking sheet. When they're all coated, move the sheet to the refrigerator or freezer to set.

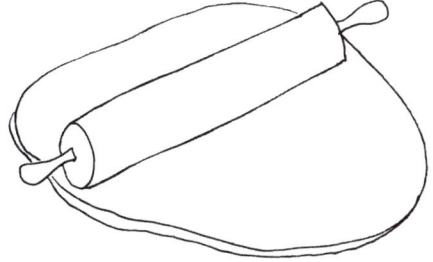

COOKIE MAGIC

Mint thins, meet chocolate chip cookie dough. You're a match made in heaven.

Mint-Thin-Stuffed Cookies

Prepare a batch of the mint thins and store them in the freezer. Then prepare a batch of the chocolate chip dough on page 43. When both are chilled, sandwich the mint cookie between 1 tablespoon each of the chocolate chip dough, then press the dough around the mint thin to cover it completely. Bake according to the chocolate chip directions.

NOTES:

Triple Chocolate Cookies

I know what you're thinking: You had me at triple chocolate. Truly, what's the fun in scrimping? After all, no recipe swap, potluck, or bake sale would be complete without someone going over-the-top chocolaty. These thrice-saturated delights aren't toothache-inducing thanks to the use of semisweet chips and bars, but they're certainly chewy and moist and have a cocoa force to be reckoned with.

PREHEAT OVEN TO 350°F

MAKES:
5 DOZEN COOKIES

1¾	cups all-purpose flour
¼	cup cocoa powder
1¾	teaspoons baking powder
¼	teaspoon salt
12	ounces semisweet chocolate, coarsely chopped
½	cup unsalted butter, at room temperature
1¼	cups dark brown sugar
¼	cup sugar
3	eggs
1½	teaspoons vanilla extract
1	cup (8 oz) semisweet chocolate chips

MIX

1. Sift the flour, cocoa powder, baking powder, and salt into a bowl and set it aside.

2. Set a small pot of water on the stove and bring it to a simmer. Place the chopped chocolate in a metal or heatproof glass bowl and set the bowl atop the pot. Stir the chocolate until it's fully melted and looks smooth. Remove from the heat.

tip

Chocolate burns easily, so make sure the bowl doesn't touch the water.

3. Cream the butter and sugars on medium speed for several minutes, until they're light and fluffy. Add the eggs and the vanilla and mix to combine. Pour in the melted chocolate (mmm) and continue beating.

4. Add the flour mixture and chocolate chips, half at a time, and mix on low speed, until just incorporated.

5. Cover the dough and refrigerate for about 15 to 20 minutes, until it's firm enough to scoop. Line several cookie sheets with parchment paper or silicone baking mats while you wait.

6. Roll the dough into 1½-inch balls and place them on the sheets about 2 inches apart. Bake for 8 to 10 minutes. They'll still appear soft, but they'll firm up once cooled. Set the sheet on a wire rack for a few minutes, then transfer the cookies directly onto the rack to cool completely.

MO' CHOCOLATE

Quadruple Chocolate Chip Cookies
Reduce the semisweet chips to ³/₄ cup, and add ¹/₂ cup white chocolate chips.

NOTES:

FANCY

65
AMARETTI

69
FRENCH
MACARONS

71
MADELEINES

67
BLACK
AND WHITE
COOKIES

63
ALFAJORES

76
PINWHEELS

79
VANILLA
MERINGUES

73
PALMIERS

Alfajores
WITH DULCE DE LECHE

Almost no one I know recognizes these treats by name. (They're pronounced *alfa-HOAR-ays*.) But when I brought them to friends and colleagues as I tested batches, the look and taste of them did trigger a few dozen "Oh, yeahs!" Good enough for me. It's not just in the name—delicate, slightly sweet alfajores have exotic appeal in taste, too. A mysterious texture blend between sandy shortbreads and cakey snickerdoodles, they've got the perfect crumby bite. The creamy, caramelly dulce de leche (literally) seals the deal.

PREHEAT OVEN TO 325°F

MAKES:
3 DOZEN COOKIES

6 tablespoons unsalted butter, at room temperature

½ cup sugar

1 cup all-purpose flour

¾ cup cornstarch

1 teaspoon baking powder

¼ teaspoon salt

1 egg

1 egg yolk

1 teaspoon vanilla extract

Store-bought dulce de leche,* for filling

Powdered sugar, for dusting

✱ Dulce de leche is similar to caramel. Splurge on a gourmet or artisanal brand, rather than a supermarket brand. It's worth it.

MIX

1. Cream the butter and sugar together for a minute or two, until they look light and fluffy.

2. In the meantime, sift the flour, cornstarch, baking powder, and salt into a bowl and set it aside.

3. Add in the egg and egg yolk one at a time, mixing after each addition. Add in the vanilla extract and mix briefly. Add in the flour mixture and mix just until the dough starts to come together.

4. Working quickly, turn out the dough and use a little heat from your hands to make it

CONTINUED

Alfajores, cont'd...

a solid ball. Pull out a large piece of plastic wrap and flatten the dough on top of it to make a disk. Double wrap it and refrigerate for 1 hour, until firm.

5. Line several cookie sheets with parchment paper or silicone mats. Roll the dough to ¼-inch thick on a lightly floured surface. Rotate the dough between rolls to make sure it's not sticking to the surface. Using a 2-inch fluted or round cutter, cut out cookies and carefully transfer them onto the sheets, placing them about 1 inch apart.

6. Chill the sheets again for about 15 to 20 minutes, until the dough is very firm. Then bake for 8 to 10 minutes, until the tops of the cookies have just firmed and bottoms are starting to color slightly. Cool the sheets on wire racks before assembling the sandwiches.

7. Drop, pipe, or spread a teaspoon of dulce de leche into the center of each cookie, then top with another. Sift powdered sugar over the assembled sandwiches.

HOMEMADE DELICIOUSNESS

Creamy dulce de leche filling isn't hard to make—it just takes time. If you have 3 hours to spare while it cooks, try it!

Dulce de leche

Bring a small pot of water to a simmer, then set 14 ounces of sweetened condensed milk into a metal bowl over the water. (Make sure the bottom of the bowl doesn't touch the water.) Cook over low heat 3 hours or until it becomes thick and dark golden, stirring occasionally to prevent the bottom from burning. Let the filling cool and thicken before assembling the cookies.

NOTES:

Amaretti
WITH CHEWY CENTERS

I fear if it weren't for their inclusion in the occasional TV recipe ("As a finishing touch, sprinkle some crushed amaretti over the top..."), these cookies would be forgotten. They shouldn't be! Amaretti are rustic, low-maintenance cousins to the trendy French macaron. But there's no tedious egg white whipping or perfect piping required—at least not in this version. I like mine just chewy enough to get a little stuck in my teeth, but crispy enough to easily dislodge with a swig of cappuccino.

PREHEAT OVEN TO 350°F

MAKES: 2-3 DOZEN COOKIES

1 cup blanched, slivered almonds
¾ cup sugar
2 egg whites, at room temperature
    pinch salt
½ teaspoon almond extract

 MIX

1. Quickly blast the almonds, the sugar, and 1 of the egg whites in a food processor. You're looking for the almonds to almost fully break down, and having the egg white in there will help form a paste. Add the second egg white, a pinch of salt, and the almond extract and puree the mixture until relatively smooth.

2. Drop the dough by teaspoonfuls onto parchment-paper-lined baking sheets at least 2 inches apart. The batter will be loose, but resist the urge to pour larger cookies—they expand!

 BAKE

3. Bake for 18 to 20 minutes, making sure to rotate sheets halfway through baking. Err on

tip

If you're using a Silpat sheet instead of parchment, these cookies tend to expand even more.

CONTINUED

Amaretti, cont'd...

the side of overcooking rather than under—it'll produce crispier edges. Cool sheets for around five minutes before transferring cookies onto wire racks to cool. If you have trouble peeling them off the parchment, slip a hand underneath the paper to help peel it away.

MAKE SANDWICH COOKIES

Double up cookies with hazelnut spread—such as Nutella—or other yummy fillings.

Hazelnut Amaretti Sandwiches

Smear about 1 tablespoon hazelnut spread on the flat side of half the cookie, top with another cookie, and press lightly to adhere.

NOTES:

Black and White Cookies

Sometimes you can't decide if you're in a chocolate or a vanilla mood. Luckily for me, you can hardly pass a bakery or lunch shop in New York City without running into a stack of giant black and white cookies. The cookie part is cakey and moist, and when the chocolate and vanilla frosting hardens, the texture is perfection.

PREHEAT OVEN TO 375°F

MAKES: 2 DOZEN COOKIES*

*Or 4 dozen minis

FANCY

4 cups cake flour
½ teaspoon baking powder
½ teaspoon salt
1 cup unsalted butter, softened
1¾ cups sugar
½ teaspoon vanilla extract
½ teaspoon lemon extract
4 egg whites
¾ cup milk
Icing (p. 68)

 MIX

1. Grease a few cookie sheets and set them aside. Sift the flour, baking powder, and salt into a medium bowl and leave it to hang out with the buttered sheets.

2. Start beating the butter on medium speed for a minute or two, until it's completely smooth. With the mixer on low speed, add the sugar in a slow stream. Cream the butter and sugar on medium-high speed for several minutes, until it's even lighter and looks fluffy. Add both extracts, then add the egg whites one at a time, mixing to combine between each addition.

 BAKE

3. Add the flour mixture and milk in alternating additions, 3 additions of each, starting with the flour mixture. Mix just until combined.

 tip

Lemon and vanilla extracts add a lovely light aroma to this cookie dough.

CONTINUED

Black and White Cookies, cont'd...

4. Drop ¼-cup-sized scoops of dough about 5 inches apart onto cookie sheets. Wet a small offset spatula or butter knife with water. Spread each cookie ball into a 3-inch round, creating as smooth a surface as possible. Continue to wet the spatula as needed to smooth each top.

For smaller ones, drop tablespoonfuls 3 inches apart.

5. Bake the cookies for 8 to 10 minutes, rotating the sheets halfway through baking, until edges just begin to turn light golden. Err on the side of less cooked here, to prevent them from stiffening beyond a soft cakelike texture. Cool the sheets on wire racks.

HOMEMADE DELICOUSNESS

Black and white cookie icing is the real deal: it's colored with cocoa, not food coloring.

6 cups powdered sugar
9 tablespoons milk (more as needed)
1½ teaspoons vanilla extract
4 tablespoons cocoa powder

Mix the powdered sugar, milk, and vanilla in a bowl until smooth. Transfer half of the icing to another bowl and add the cocoa powder. Be sure to mix until any chocolaty lumps have disappeared. Using the small offset spatula or butter knife again, spread the chocolate icing on half of the cookie. Follow with the vanilla icing on the other half. Let iced cookies set for 30 minutes back on the wire racks.

NOTES:

FANCY

French Macarons
WITH CLASSIC ALMOND FILLING

You will be baking royalty once these delicate show-stoppers make their entrance during the coffee course: They're like fancy punctuation to a meal. Adding bright, playful colors with a few drops of food dye makes them an exceptionally stunning treat.

PREHEAT OVEN TO 375°F

MAKES:
1½ DOZEN COOKIES

Shelling:

1	cup	almond meal or finely ground blanched almonds
1¼	cups	powdered sugar
¼	cup	sugar
3		egg whites

Filling:

¼	cup	unsalted butter, at room temperature
¼	cup	powdered sugar
2	tablespoons	almond meal or ground, blanched almonds

MIX

1. First make the shells: Grind the almonds and powdered sugar in a food processor until superfine. Sift the mixture, tossing out any big pieces left behind.

2. Whip the egg whites on medium-low speed until foamy. Bump up the speed to medium and slowly stream in the sugar, pausing to let it incorporate, until the egg whites form soft to medium peaks. You can test this by pulling a spoon through the egg whites—the peak should stick almost straight up, but then droop downward at the end. Remove the bowl and gently fold in the almond meal mixture a little at a time.

BAKE

3. Fit a pastry bag with a large, plain tip. Fill the bag about halfway with the macaron batter. Working on a parchment-paper-lined cookie

tip

On humid, wet days, macarons might droop a bit and get sticky. You'll have the best luck making them on dry days.

CONTINUED

sheet, pipe small disks (about 1½ to 2 inches) about 2 inches apart. Don't worry if the dough seems difficult to pipe at first—it will soften as you go. Set the piped creations aside for 30 minutes for the tops to set slightly. When you've got a few minutes to go, preheat the oven.

4. Bake for 10 minutes, turning the oven down to 300°F for the last 5 minutes. The cookies will taste delicious now, but if you plan to fill them, wait until they've cooled.

5. To make the filling: Beat the butter until smooth. Add the powdered sugar and almond meal and mix until they're combined. Pair up the cooled macarons, matching by similar size. Spread a thin layer of the filling (about ⅛-inch thick) onto one flat side of each pair. Create a sandwich with the other macaron.

 **tip** To achieve perfectly smooth tops, release pressure on the piping bag and finish with a tight swirl of the wrist before pulling the bag upward and away. Don't worry if the first few don't come out perfectly: you have a whole batch to practice on! If you're really unhappy with them, just scrape the dough off the cookie sheet, add it back into the pastry bag, and try again.

FLAVORS TO TRY

Blackberry Macarons
Mix 1½ tablespoons strained blackberry puree into the batter, plus a few drops deep purple gel food coloring. Fill with blackberry jam.

Salted Cashew Macarons
Substitute an equal amount of finely ground unsalted cashews for the almond meal, and sprinkle the tops with coarse salt. Fill with chocolate ganache (recipe on page 141).

Caramel Corn Macarons
Add a few drops egg-yellow gel food coloring to the macaron batter. Fill the end result with store-bought dulce de leche.

NOTES:

Madeleines

The honey flavor is my favorite part of these spongy, cakey desserts. You do need the traditional pan to make them—kitchen stores sell inexpensive small ones, so make the investment. As you would if baking a cake, be sure to check that the centers are fully cooked before removing them from the oven.

PREHEAT OVEN TO 400°F

MAKES: 2 DOZEN COOKIES

¾ cup unsalted butter
4 eggs
½ cup sugar
¼ cup honey
1 teaspoon vanilla extract
1½ cups all-purpose flour
2 teaspoons baking powder
¼ teaspoon salt

 MIX

1. Melt the butter and let it cool slightly. Combine the eggs, sugar, honey, and vanilla together and whisk until the mixture is thick and foamy.

2. Sift the flour, baking powder, and salt over the egg mixture and carefully fold it in with a rubber spatula. Add the melted butter and fold that in gently, too. Cover the batter and refrigerate at least 8 hours.

 BAKE

3. Butter the madeleine tray and spoon in the batter until each mold is about three-fourths full. Bake for 5 to 7 minutes, until golden brown. Let cool for a few minutes in the tray, and the rest of the way on a rack.

 tip

Chilling the batter helps Madeleines form their distinctive "bump."

 CONTINUED

Madeleines, cont'd...

ADD A TWIST

This sunny lemon glaze gives madeleines a lovely flavor and a pretty finish. Of course, if you don't love citrus, there's always chocolate.

Lemony Glaze

Mix 1¼ cups powdered sugar with 1 tablespoon fresh-squeezed lemon juice and mix (patiently) until a thick glaze starts to form. If the mixture is not loose enough for dunking, add more lemon juice, a half teaspoon at a time. If mixture gets too loose (in which case it won't be thick enough to set), add more powdered sugar and continue mixing.

Drizzle over cookies or dunk them ⅓ inch, one at a time.

NOTES:

Palmiers

Once you know the hours of work that go into making a palmier from scratch—namely, the puff pastry—you'll never overlook one again on a bakery counter. You shouldn't anyway: They're gorgeous and simple and have the perfect sweetness-to-crunch ratio. (The sugar bakes into the dough, caramelizing as it cooks. Heaven.) The chef who taught me how to make them may cringe at my use of store-bought puff pastry, but it's a cheat that's sure to put these beautiful treats into more home baker's ovens, so I may just get away with it.

PREHEAT OVEN TO 375°F

MAKES: 2 DOZEN COOKIES

1 1-pound sheet frozen puff pastry

1½ cups sugar

1 egg

MIX

1. Let the puff pastry defrost slightly, so it's still firm but not greasy or soft. Sprinkle about half the sugar onto a clean work surface and lay the dough on top. Sprinkle about half the remaining sugar on top of the dough.

2. Working gently but quickly, use a rolling pin to form the puff pastry into a ¼-inch-thick rectangle, pressing to help the sugar adhere. Pause every few rolls to add more sugar to both sides of the dough. Keep rolling. You want the dough to be as sugary as possible—it will all caramelize into a beautiful brown shade later.

3. Beat the egg with a tablespoon of water.

CONTINUED

Palmiers, cont'd...

4. Fold the two long sides of the dough rectangle toward each other, stopping halfway toward the center. Fold them both toward the center once more.

5. Brush the exposed sides of the dough with the egg wash. Working carefully to match up the sides as evenly as possible, fold the dough in half again, forming a long tube. Sprinkle any remaining sugar on top, and use the rolling pin to pack down the dough ever so slightly, so it sticks together. Let the dough chill for 15 to 20 minutes in the fridge to firm up a bit.

BAKE 6. Line a baking sheet with parchment paper. Use a sharp knife to cut the chilled log into ¼-inch-thick slices. Lay them on the baking sheet at least 2 inches apart. Bake for about 12 to 14 minutes, until the underside of the palmiers looks golden brown. Use a spatula to flip them over and then place back in the oven for another 2 to 3 minutes, until both sides are evenly cooked and crisped. Remove and cool on wire racks.

VARIATION

Lemony Palmiers
Add the zest of 1 large lemon to the sugar before pressing it into the dough.

NOTES:

FANCY

Pinwheels

Chocolate and vanilla clearly have their own fan clubs when it comes to sweets, but the swirl gets a serious shortage of love. In this case, it creates a childhood throwback chocolate-milky taste. I rarely see these cookies baked outside of cafés and shops, but there's really no good reason. You split one simple sugar dough in half to form two flavors, then roll both together and slice into disks. End of duties, beginning of snack time.

PREHEAT OVEN TO 350°F

MAKES:
4 DOZEN COOKIES

3 cups all-purpose flour
½ teaspoon baking powder
¼ teaspoon salt
1 cup unsalted butter,
   at room temperature
1½ cups sugar
2 eggs
2 teaspoons vanilla extract
2 tablespoons cocoa powder

MIX

1. Get to work sifting the flour, baking powder, and salt into a bowl. Set it aside for the moment.

2. Cream together the butter and sugar for several minutes, until light and fluffy. Add the eggs and the vanilla and mix until incorporated.

3. Start tipping in the flour a third at a time; stop mixing when it's just combined.

4. When the dough forms, divide it into two parts. Reserve one half in plastic wrap and keep it in the fridge. Mix the cocoa powder into the other half using a spatula. Form the chocolate dough into a disk, wrap in plastic wrap, and chill both doughs in the fridge for at least 1 hour, until firm.

5. Roll out the chocolate dough to about ¼-inch thickness, using just a little flour as needed. Move it to a large piece of parchment

paper. Do the same with the vanilla dough, flattening them to around the same height and dimension. Place the vanilla dough on top of the chocolate and run a rolling pin lightly over the two doughs to press them together. Trim the doughs into a rectangle shape so they each have the same edges.

6. Starting at one of the short ends, carefully roll the dough up into a log, using the parchment paper to help. Wrap it tightly in plastic wrap or parchment paper and chill for at least an hour. Do the same with the reserved pieces of dough.

tip

Don't worry if the dough cracks slightly. You won't notice when they're baked.

BAKE 7. Line a few cookie sheets with parchment paper. Unwrap the log and slice it into cookies about ¼-inch thick using a very sharp knife. Lay the cookies on the sheets about 2 inches apart.

8. Bake for 10 to 12 minutes, until you start seeing hints of the edges turning golden. Remove and let cool for a minute, then spatula to a wire rack.

VARIATION

Cut the pinwheel log on a long bias for a stretchier spiral.

NOTES:

FANCY

Vanilla Meringues

Every part of making this recipe is exhilarating—from waiting for the egg whites to firm up in your mixer bowl to dolloping the thick marshmallowy batter onto the baking sheet. It's like a grown-up art project. And the results are so sophisticated.

PREHEAT OVEN TO 225°F

MAKES: 1 DOZEN COOKIES

3   egg whites,
        at room temperature
    Pinch salt
¼   teaspoon cream of tartar
¼   teaspoon vanilla extract
1   cup sugar

 MIX

1. Start by slowly whisking the egg whites until foamy. Add salt, cream of tartar, and vanilla and whisk faster until soft peaks form.

2. With the mixer motor still running, add the sugar slowly—tip in about 1 tablespoon every 5 seconds. Halfway through the sugar, switch the motor to high and continue beating until it starts to look very stiff and glossy, about 3 minutes. (Test by rubbing a little bit of the meringue between two fingers. If you can still feel lots of sugar grains, it's not ready.)

 BAKE

3. Line a cookie sheet with parchment paper and dab a little meringue batter under the corners of the paper to help secure it. Pipe the batter onto cookie sheets using a pastry, bag fitted with a ½-inch tip.

tip

If you don't have a pastry bag, just drop 2-inch mounds of meringue from a large spoon onto the sheet.

 CONTINUED

4. Bake for 1 hour 15 minutes to 1 hour and 30 minutes, rotating the sheets halfway through baking, until the outsides of the meringues look firm and dry but not too browned. Turn off the oven and leave them inside for another 20 minutes.

MERINGUES FOR CHOCOLATE LOVERS

Serve a variety of vanilla and chocolate meringues for a gourmet spread.

Chocolate Meringues

$1/2$ cup sugar
$1/4$ cup powdered sugar
1 tablespoon plus 1 teaspoon cocoa powder

Reduce the sugar in Step 2 to $1/2$ cup. When you're done whipping the sugar and whites, sift the powdered sugar and the cocoa together into a bowl and gently fold them into the meringue until incorporated.

Chocolate Chip Meringues

Sprinkle two handfuls of mini chocolate chips into the fluffy egg whites and gently fold them in with a spatula.

Cocoa Nib Meringues

Toss a palmful of cocoa nibs into the fluffy egg whites and gently fold them in with a spatula.

NOTES:

NOTES:

FRUITY

A COOKIE A DAY KEEPS DARK SKIES AWAY

94
LINZER COOKIES

99
RUGELACH

87
DRIED-FRUIT COOKIES

84
COCONUT MACAROONS

91
LEMON
CHEWIES

97
OATMEAL RAISIN
COOKIES

101
THUMBPRINTS

89
FIG
BARS

Coconut Macaroons

Buy a sack of shredded coconut once, and you'll always have the ingredients for these cookies on hand. They're quick and easy and perfect for snacking. My girlfriends and I make them impromptu while watching (embarrassingly bad) TV.

PREHEAT OVEN TO 350°F

MAKES:
2 DOZEN COOKIES

3 cups sweetened coconut flakes

4 egg whites

1 cup sugar

Pinch salt

1½ teaspoons vanilla extract

Flour, for rolling

MIX

1. Combine the coconut, egg whites, sugar, and salt in a small saucepan and set over medium-low heat. The ingredients will begin to melt and loosen up at first, but after a few minutes they'll tighten up again. That's because some of the moisture is evaporating. Continue to let cook until the batter looks firm enough to hold shape, about 10 minutes total.

tip

At this point, you can also chill the batter for a day or two.

2. Remove from the heat and stir in the vanilla. Transfer to a bowl to cool to room temperature.

3. Line several cookie sheets with parchment paper or silicone baking mats. Run a spoon into the batter to gather about 1 to 2 tablespoons of the mix. Then, working with fingers that have been dipped in just a little bit of flour, form the coconut into little domes and set them on the cookie sheets. The cookies won't expand, so you only need to space them about 1 inch apart.

BAKE

4. Bake cookies 13 to 15 minutes, until the tops have started to turn golden brown. Try not to let them overbake—just go for a little golden color on the outsides—so they don't lose their lovable moist, chewy texture.

5. Let cool completely on the sheets, then gently peel them off.

DO THE DIP

These chewy coconutty cookies are delicious dunked in chocolate.

Chocolate-Dipped Macaroons
Follow the directions for melting chocolate on page 147, steps 5 and 6 (bittersweet or semisweet will do), and dunk the bottoms of macaroons in the chocolate. Let cool on a wire rack or parchment-lined baking sheet.

NOTES:

FRUITY

Dried-Fruit Cookies
WITH CINNAMON

If dried fruit reminds you of your grandmother, or a health food store, let's toss away that association, stat. These sweet, cinnamony cookies are just the thing to help. With jewel-toned flecks of fruits like cranberries, dates, prunes, and apricots running through a cinnamony dough, they'll win your heart—and a place in your holiday cookie roster—before you even have time to realize that, yes, I just said prunes.

PREHEAT OVEN TO 375°F

MAKES: 2½ DOZEN COOKIES

6 tablespoons unsalted butter, at room temperature

½ cup sugar

1 egg

2 tablespoons sour cream

1½ cups all-purpose flour

¼ teaspoon baking soda

¼ teaspoon salt

½ teaspoon cinnamon

½ cup plus 2 tablespoons ground or finely chopped fruit such as raisins, apricots, cranberries, dates and prunes

Sugar, for rolling

MIX

1. Cream together the butter and sugar until light and fluffy. Add the egg and mix again to incorporate. Add the sour cream and mix until no traces of white remain.

2. Sift the flour, baking soda, salt, and cinnamon together. Pour in the flour mixture half at a time, beating until it's fully mixed in. Then stir in the dried fruit pieces with a spoon.

3. Wrap the dough in plastic wrap and refrigerate 1 hour.

BAKE

4. Roll 1-inch balls and place them 2 inches apart on a lightly greased or parchment-paper-lined cookie sheet. Roll them in the sugar, place them on the cookie sheets about 2 inches

CONTINUED

Dried-Fruit Cookies, cont'd...

apart, and flatten them (a good amount—they'll rise) using two fingers. Bake the cookies until they fully set up, 10 to 12 minutes.

TRY ROLLING INSTEAD

Turn these into sliced cookies instead of drop-style. Chilled in your fridge or freezer, logs of cookie dough are perfect for slicing and baking cookies for a quick snack.

Rolled Icebox Cookies

Roll the dough into 1 big log (about 2 inches in diameter) or 2 small logs. Wrap the logs in plastic wrap and then in parchment paper, securing the ends for a tight seal. Freeze for 15 to 20 minutes or up to 2 weeks. Remove and slice into ¼-inch-thick cookies. Bake as instructed.

This technique works for most cookie doughs.

NOTES:

Fig Bars
WITH ORANGE ZEST

I patted myself on the back for this recipe, because it tastes startlingly close to the store-bought version. I kept the orange peel to a subtle amount for that reason, but if you're a fan, kick it up a notch or two.

PREHEAT OVEN TO 375°F

MAKES: 16 SLICES

½ cup unsalted butter, at room temperature

1 cup light brown sugar

1 egg

¾ teaspoon vanilla extract

1 teaspoon orange zest

2 cups plus 2 tablespoons all-purpose flour

½ teaspoon baking soda

¼ teaspoon salt

For the filling:

1¼ cups dried figs, chopped

¼ cup sugar

MIX

1. Cream the butter and brown sugar on medium speed for several minutes until light and fluffy. Add the egg, vanilla, and orange zest and mix until combined. Sift the flour, baking soda, and salt into a bowl and add it gradually to the butter mixture. Beat just until combined. Turn out the dough onto a piece of plastic wrap. Flatten it into a disk, wrap it tightly in plastic wrap, and refrigerate for 1 hour.

2. In the meantime, make the filling. Heat the figs, sugar, and 1 cup of water until the mixture reaches a boil. Then lower the heat and cook until it starts to look jammy. Set it aside to cool.

CONTINUED

Fig Bars, cont'd...

BAKE

3. Roll out half the dough on a lightly floured surface into 8-by-13-inch rectangle (it should be about ⅛-inch thick). Transfer the dough to a piece of parchment paper and trim 1 inch off each of the edges to form straight lines.

4. Spread half the figgy filling lengthwise down the middle third of the dough. Fold one-third of the dough over the filling (use the parchment to help guide your fold evenly). Repeat with the other third of the dough, letting it overlap the first folded piece by about ¾ inch. Press the layers together gently to seal the seam. Repeat with the second half of the dough and the rest of the filling.

5. Line a cookie sheet with parchment paper and place both logs onto it, seam-side down and about 4 inches apart. Chill in the fridge at least 20 minutes.

6. Bake for 20 to 23 minutes, until the logs are golden brown and feel firm. Cool completely on a wire rack before cutting into generous 1½-inch-wide slices with a serrated knife.

MORE TO TRY

Figs aren't the only fruits that are delicious in bars.

Maple Date Bars
Replace the dried figs with dried dates, and substitute 2 tablespoons maple syrup for the 3 tablespoons granulated sugar.

NOTES:

Lemon Chewies
WITH HONEY

Anything I've ever baked with loads of honey and salt has come out incredible. When I added lemon to the mix, it took this dough to a whole new level. I like these cookies to be just an inch in diameter, since they pack a sweet, lemony punch. Between their teeny size and the back-of-the cheek pucker you get from biting into one, they really make you feel like a kid again.

PREHEAT OVEN TO 350°F

MAKES:
3 DOZEN COOKIES

2 cups all-purpose flour

1 teaspoon baking powder

1 teaspoon kosher salt

½ cup unsalted butter, at room temperature

½ cup sugar

½ teaspoon lemon zest

1 egg

⅓ cup honey

MIX

1. Sift together the flour, baking powder, and salt into a bowl and set it aside.

2. Cream the butter and sugar until they look light and fluffy. Add the lemon zest and mix to incorporate.

3. In a separate bowl, crack in the egg and add the honey. Stir them together until they're fairly well mixed. Then add it to the butter mixture and beat until combined. Add the flour mixture a third at a time and let it mix in fully each time before adding the next batch; you'll see the dough start to come together. Blend just until it looks smooth.

BAKE

4. Lightly grease a cookie sheet. Then scoop teaspoons of the dough and roll them gently

CONTINUED

FRUITY

Lemon Chewies, cont'd...

into little balls. Place them on the sheets about 2 inches apart and flatten slightly with the tips of fingers or a fork. Bake for 10 to 12 minutes, until cookies are set and bottoms are golden brown.

Flour the fork if it sticks.

ADD A GLAZE

This light sweet glaze adds a pretty finish to Lemon Chewies or any other cookie.

Simple Glaze

Mix 1¼ cups powdered sugar with 1 tablespoon water and mix (patiently) until a thick glaze starts to form. If the mixture is not runny enough, add more water, a half teaspoon at a time. If mixture gets too loose (in which case it will run off the cookie and not set), add more powdered sugar and continue mixing. Drizzle over the cookies with a spoon and let dry.

NOTES:

FRUITY

Linzer Cookies
WITH JAM WINDOWS

I can't help it: these bakery classics make me think of the holidays. Festive rings, glistening jams, and a dusting of powdered sugar. But, really, they're wonderful for giving you that snowy-morning feeling any time of year. The minute the dark, smoky spices hit the fluffy flour and create that speckled batter, I start to get excited. If you're like me, the finished look is almost as important as the finished taste. Save them for a day when you have a little time to linger over an artful assembly.

PREHEAT OVEN TO 350°F

MAKES:
2½ DOZEN COOKIES

1¼ cups hazelnuts

2¾ cups all-purpose flour

1 teaspoon cinnamon

¼ teaspoon ground cloves

½ teaspoon baking powder

¼ teaspoon salt

1 cup unsalted butter,
　　at room temperature

½ cup sugar

1 egg

½ cup raspberry or apricot jam,
　　for filling

　Powdered sugar for dusting
　　(optional)

MIX

1. In a food processor, grind the hazelnuts with the flour to make a fine meal. Combine the mixture with the spices, baking powder, and salt in a bowl and set it aside.

2. In a mixer, cream the butter and sugar on medium speed for a few minutes, until they look light and fluffy. Add the egg and mix until combined. Add the hazelnut mixture and beat it in slowly until large crumbs form.

3. Turn out the dough onto a clean surface and form it into a flat rectangle. Aim for about 1 inch of thickness. Wrap it in plastic and refrigerate for about 2 hours, or until it's good and firm.

4. Line a few cookie sheets with parchment paper to get ready for baking. Roll out the dough to ⅛-inch thick. Cut out shapes with a 2-inch cookie cutter. Use a smaller cutter to make holes in half the cookies. Place them on parchment-lined sheets about 1-inch apart; chill on the sheets about 15 minutes before baking.

6. Bake 12 to 14 minutes or until cookies turn golden brown. Let them cool completely on wire racks, then fill with jam. Top with a sprinkling of powdered sugar, if you like.

MORE TO TRY

These classic cookies are easy to adapt with different nuts in the dough or different fillings sandwiched in between.

Blueberry Linzers
Switch up the jams for an easy berry variation.

Pecan Linzers
Swap hazelnuts for toasted pecans.

NOTES:

Oatmeal Raisin Cookies
WITH PLENTY O' RAISINS

Thanks to the sweet, fat raisins stirred into every bite and their thick, oaty chew, I've convinced myself that these quintessential cookies are healthy. (Shhh.) For some reason, they always tempt me to keep them in the oven longer—don't fall for it. They're best when they're good and chewy, barely starting to crisp on the outside.

PREHEAT OVEN TO 350°F

MAKES:
2 DOZEN COOKIES

½ cup unsalted butter, at room temperature
⅔ cup light brown sugar
1 egg
1 teaspoon vanilla extract
¾ cup all-purpose flour
½ teaspoon baking soda
½ teaspoon salt
½ teaspoon ground cinnamon
1½ cups old-fashioned rolled oats or quick-cooking oats
⅔ cup raisins

 MIX

1. Cream together the butter and sugar on medium speed for a few minutes until the mixture is light and fluffy. Add the egg and vanilla and mix a bit more.

2. Sift the flour, baking soda, salt, and cinnamon into a bowl. Pour in the flour mixture and run the mixer motor on low, just to work it in. Stir in the oats and raisins with a spoon.

 BAKE

3. Scoop out tablespoon-sized balls of dough onto parchment-paper-lined cookie sheets about 2 inches apart.

4. Bake for 12 to 14 minutes, rotating cookie sheets halfway through baking. Let cool and enjoy.

 tip

For a taller, chewier oatmeal cookie, chill the dough for 10 to 15 minutes, or until a little firmer before baking.

FRUITY

CONTINUED

Oatmeal Raisin Cookies, cont'd...

MORE MIX-INS TO TRY

- Dried Cherries
- White Chocolate Chips
- Chocolate-Covered Raisins
- Toasted Almonds
- Toffee Bits
- Dark Chocolate Chunks
- Cranberries
- Chopped Soft Caramels
- Peanut Butter Chips

NOTES:

Rugelach
WITH CINNAMON-RAISIN FILLING

Whoever invented this combination was a matchmaking genius: tender, creamy dough oozing with perfectly caramelized cinammon-sugary goodness. Like rugelach's other stuffed and rolled cousins (think ravioli, dim sum, and croissants), the extra effort it takes to make them is *so worth it*. Work in phases to keep it breezy: first the smooth white dough, which keeps for a couple of days in the fridge, then the nut-flecked stuffing, which can be mixed mere moments before you put them in the oven. When they come out, browned and beautiful, I guarantee you'll be a proud parent.

PREHEAT OVEN TO 350°F

MAKES:
2 DOZEN COOKIES

4 ounces cream cheese, at room temperature

½ cup unsalted butter, at room temperature

1 cup all-purpose flour

1½ teaspoons sugar

⅛ teaspoon salt

Filling:

½ cup pecans, chopped

¼ cup dark or golden raisins

½ teaspoon cinnamon, plus 1 teaspoon more for sprinkling

¼ cup sugar, plus 3 tablespoons more for sprinkling

Egg wash*

✱ 1 egg beaten with 1 tablespoon milk or water

MIX

1. Beat the cream cheese for a minute until it smooths out. Add the butter and beat the two together for another minute, until they combine and look fluffy.

2. Mix together the flour, sugar, and salt and add them to the cream cheese mixture on low speed until incorporated. Stop when the dough looks mealy.

3. Form the dough together with your hands and divide it in half to form two disks.

4. Wrap each disk in plastic wrap and chill for at least an hour.

CONTINUED

FRUITY

Rugelach, cont'd...

5. When you're ready to bake, add the pecans, raisins, cinnamon, and sugar to a food processor and pulse a few times until the pecans and raisins are finely chopped. Remove one of the discs of dough from the fridge and roll it out onto a floured surface to form a thin circle, about 9 inches in diameter and ¼-inch thick. Cover it all over with the filling like a pizza, leaving a thin border on the outside rim, and press gently.

Don't worry about rolling them super tightly. They get a little doughier when they bake, so a little slack won't hurt.

6. Slice the dough into about 12 wedges, like you would a pizza (cut it into quarters, then cut each quarter into thirds). Starting from the wider edge (where the "crust" would be) and working gently but quickly, roll each rugelach from the wide end toward the pointy end.

7 Place them, pointy parts tucked under, on parchment-paper lined baking sheets and chill for another 10 minutes. (I like to use this time to clean up.)

8. You're almost there! For the final step, brush some of the egg wash over the tops of the cookies. Mix together the remaining cinnamon and sugar and sprinkle it over the tops. Bake for 15 to 18 minutes, until lightly browned. Let cool on a wire rack. Sweet victory.

FRUITY

MAKE IT FRUITY

Apricot Rugelach

Fill the dough with apricot jam instead of the raisin mixture. Brush more jam over the top just before baking, and sprinkle lightly with cinnamon and sugar.

NOTES:

Thumbprints
WITH BERRY JAM

I have to thank my older sister for inspiring this recipe. The homemade batch she brought to our Christmas dinner last year got so many oohs and ahhs, I had to step up my thumbprint game. In the spirit of friendly sibling rivalry, I skipped asking for her recipe and instead tried to one-up her with my own. Call it a tie, sis?

PREHEAT OVEN TO 350°F

MAKES: 4 DOZEN COOKIES

1 cup unsalted butter, at room temperature

²/₃ cup sugar

2 egg yolks

2 cups all-purpose flour

½ teaspoon kosher salt

1 cup assorted fruit jams*

✳ If the preserves are too thick or sticky to spoon easily into the holes, just melt it a bit in a small saucepan.

tip

If the jam centers don't look full enough, drop in more jam while cookies are still hot from the oven.

 MIX

1. Cream together the butter and sugar for several minutes, until they look light and fluffy. Add the egg yolks and beat until combined.

2. Mix together flour and salt in a separate bowl. Gradually pour the dry ingredients into the wet and beat until smooth.

 BAKE

3. Tear off small chunks of the dough and roll them quickly between your palms to form ¾-inch balls. Before putting each one onto the baking sheet, press your thumb or the back of a wooden spoon into the center to make a hole large enough to fit about 1 teaspoon of filling.

4. Place the cookies on parchment-lined sheets and drop in the jam right from the teaspoon. Bake for 12 to 15 minutes, until cookies are set but not yet browning. Let cool completely before storing.

CONTINUED ➡

MAKE 'EM YOUR WAY

Fill these little cookies with anything you like. Their simple flavor and shape adapt well to almost any filling.

Lemon Thumbprints
Replace the jam with store-bought lemon curd.

Chocolate Thumbprints
Bake cookies without any filling. Then drop in teaspoonfuls of prepared chocolate pudding, chocolate frosting or ganache while they're still warm.

NOTES:

FRUITY

SPICY

112
GINGERBREAD
MEN

107
CARDAMOM
COOKIES

109
GINGERSNAPS

117
MOLASSES SPICE
COOKIES

115
GREEN TEA COOKIES

119
SALT-AND-
PEPPER COOKIES

123
SNICKERDOODLES

Cardamom Cookies
WITH SLIVERED ALMONDS

These crisp afternoon treats have more than just a pretty face. The lemony, woodsy scent of savory cardamom lures you in.

PREHEAT OVEN TO 375°F

MAKES: 3½ DOZEN COOKIES

⅔ cup unsalted butter, at room temperature

1 cup sugar

2 eggs

2½ cups all-purpose flour

2 teaspoons baking powder

¾ teaspoon salt

1 teaspoon ground cardamom

Small cup of milk or 2 egg whites, for brushing

Slivered almonds, lightly crushed

MIX

1. Cream the butter and sugar together until they're light and fluffy. Add the eggs and beat until a smooth mixture forms.

2. Sift together the flour, baking powder, and salt and stir in the cardamom. Add the dry ingredients half at a time and beat until incorporated. Turn out the dough onto a clean surface and form it into a disk. Chill for 1 hour in the fridge (or 20 minutes in the freezer).

BAKE

3. Cut the dough into quarters and set one quarter on a lightly floured work surface. Keep the other 3 in the fridge while you work. Roll out the dough to ¼-inch thick, cut out the cookies, and place them on cookie sheets about 1 inch apart. Brush the top of the

CONTINUED

SPICY

Cardamom Cookies, cont'd...

cookies with the milk or lightly beaten egg whites and sprinkle with the crushed almonds. Bake until golden brown, 8 to 10 minutes.

TRY OTHER SPICES

Cardamom is lovely, but this recipe adapts well to other flavors, too.

Caraway Cookies
Omit the ground cardamom and add 1 tablespoon crushed caraway seeds to the dough.

NOTES:

Gingersnaps
DUSTED IN SUGAR

Anytime of day, anytime of year, this is a cookie that calls my name. Reminiscent of graham crackers in flavor, it's a treat that makes the perfect breakfast (albeit one your mom would never approve), snacktime or end to a meal. I dream about floating one in a glass of milk for dessert before dinner is even over. By the time you've rolled a few of the snaps in the sugar, you'll start to feel the same.

PREHEAT OVEN TO 350°F

MAKES:
4-5 DOZEN COOKIES

3 cups all-purpose flour

2½ teaspoons baking soda

1½ teaspoons ground ginger

1 teaspoon ground cinnamon

¼ teaspoon black pepper

¼ teaspoon salt

1 cup unsalted butter, at room temperature

¼ cup sugar, plus extra for rolling

¼ cup light brown sugar

1 egg

$1/3$ cup molasses

MIX

1. Sift the flour, baking soda, spices, and salt into a bowl and set it aside.

2. Cream the butter and sugars on medium speed for several minutes until smooth, light, and fluffy.

3. Beat in the egg, then the molasses, and mix again. The dough will start turning a lovely brown color.

4. Mix in the flour mixture one-third at a time. Turn out the dough onto a lightly floured surface. Using a big piece of parchment paper, roll the dough into one 18-inch log or two 9-inch logs—they're much easier to handle. Tuck the parchment around the ends and stick dough in the fridge for 30 minutes, or until firm enough to slice.

tip

To keep sliced cookies round, rotate the dough log on the cutting board a tiny bit each time you slice. Don't trust your skills? Just roll it out to $1/8$-inch and use a cookie cutter.

CONTINUED

Gingersnaps, cont'd...

5. Grease several cookie sheets. Fill a small bowl with the extra sugar. Using a sharp knife, cut slices ¼- to ⅜-inch thick. Coat the slices in sugar and place on the sheets about 2 inches apart.

6. Bake for 6 to 10 minutes, until set but not browned. Cool sheets for a few minutes before moving cookies to a wire rack.

tip

For chewy cookies, remove them from the oven a minute or two earlier, when each cookie is just barely holding its shape when nudged.

MORE TO TRY

These crisp gingery little cookies are good for sandwiching, stacking, and topping with gooey treats.

Gingersnap S'mores

Sandwich two gingersnaps around a small dollop of marshmallow fluff, then dunk in melted and slightly cooled milk chocolate. (Follow the chocolate dunking recipe on page 147, step 6, but substitute milk or semisweet chocolate.)

Gingersnap Sandwiches with Dulche de Leche

Gently spread about 1 tablespoon of store-bought dulce de leche onto the flat side of one cookie; top with another cookie. Dust lightly with powdered sugar, if desired.

NOTES:

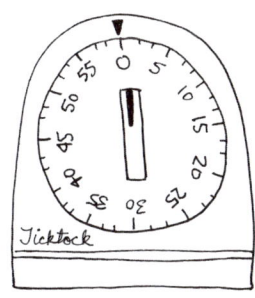

SPICY

Gingerbread Men

These guys aren't just for decorating. Softer, chewier, and made with more bright ginger and less smokey clove than most gingerbread men, they're tasty, too.

PREHEAT OVEN TO 350°F

MAKES:
2½ DOZEN COOKIES

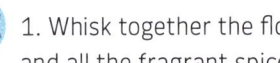

3½ cups all-purpose flour

1½ teaspoons baking soda

1 teaspoon coarse salt

1½ teaspoons ground ginger

1¼ teaspoons ground cinnamon

½ teaspoon ground allspice

¼ teaspoon ground cloves

1 cup unsalted butter,
     at room temperature

1 cup dark brown sugar

½ cup granulated sugar

1 egg

¼ cup molasses

MIX

1. Whisk together the flour, baking soda, salt, and all the fragrant spices and set them aside.

2. Beat the butter and sugars together until they look fluffy. Then add the egg and pour in the molasses, and beat again to incorporate. Stop to scrape down the sticky sides of the bowl as needed.

3. Add the flour mixture, a third at a time, mixing until it's worked in. Turn out the beautiful brown dough onto a piece of plastic wrap, gather it into a disc, and refrigerate for a minimum of 2 hours (overnight is even better).

4. Remove the dough and cut the disc in half. Reserve one-half in the fridge, and let the other sit out for a few minutes until it's softened slightly and easier to roll. On a floured surface, roll it out to ¼-inch thick.

BAKE 5. Cut out shapes with cookie cutters and slide them onto parchment-paper-lined cookie sheets. To keep the cut-out shape as perfect as possible, stick the whole cookie sheet in the freezer for about 10 minutes. Bake until cookies appear firm and like they're just starting to crisp, about 12 to 15 minutes.

tip

They'll crisp up
more as they cool.

MAKE 'EM YOUR WAY

If you don't like to get out your rolling pin, try drop cookies instead. They're thicker and chewier than flat gingerbread men.

Gingerbread Drop Cookies
Skip the rolling and cutting. Form the chilled dough into 1-inch balls and roll them in granulated sugar. Place on a baking sheet about 1½ inches apart and bake until set but still soft.

NOTES:

SPICY

Green Tea Cookies

These radiant treats make the most beautiful eye candy. They're made with matcha, or pure Japanese green tea powder, which has a bright, slightly bitter flavor.

PREHEAT OVEN TO 350°F

MAKES:
2 DOZEN COOKIES

¾ cup powdered sugar

1 tablespoons plus 1 teaspoon pure matcha powder*

½ cup plus 2 tablespoons unsalted butter, at room temperature

3 egg yolks

1¾ cups all-purpose flour

Pinch salt

Sugar, for dusting (optional)

✱ Bright green matcha powder—made with finely ground green tea leaves—can be found in the tea aisle of most grocery stores.

MIX

1. Mix together the powdered sugar and matcha powder. Add in the butter and beat it all together until smooth and spinach green. Add the egg yolks and beat until mostly incorporated, scraping down the green, sticky stuff off the side of the bowl, as needed.

2. Pour in the flour and pinch of salt, half at a time, and beat to combine. It will take a minute for the flour to absorb into the dough, so don't rush it. Once all the flour is in, use your hands to check for particularly gooey or dry sections of the dough (it will still look very crumby); if you find any, keep mixing.

3. Use the warmth of your hands to pull the dough together into a ball. Lay out the ball onto a piece of plastic wrap, seal it up, and form the ball into a flattened disk. Chill it until firm enough to roll, about 30 minutes to 1 hour.

CONTINUED

SPICY

Green Tea Cookies, cont'd...

 4. When you're ready to bake, roll out the dough to about ½-inch thick. Drop the cookies in the sugar (if using) and flip them to coat both sides. Set them on a parchment-paper-lined cookie sheet and bake 12 to 15 minutes, until barely starting to turn golden. Cool on wire racks.

ADD A LITTLE KICK

Ginger and green tea are a refreshing flavor combination.

Ginger-Dusted Green Tea Cookies
Sprinkle a healthy dusting of ground ginger and granulated sugar atop cookies before baking.

NOTES:

SPICY

Molasses Spice Cookies
WITH FRESHLY GROUND SPICES

These wintry cookies get overlooked for being too traditional. But when you're craving a gingery treat, they're softer and chewier than their spicy crisp gingersnap cousins, and twice the size.

PREHEAT OVEN TO 325°F

MAKES:
1 DOZEN COOKIES

2¹⁄₃ cups all-purpose flour

2 teaspoons baking soda

½ teaspoon salt

1 teaspoon ground cinnamon

1½ teaspoons ground ginger

½ teaspoon freshly ground cloves

¼ teaspoon freshly ground allspice

¾ cup unsalted butter, at room temperature

½ cup dark brown sugar

½ cup sugar, plus extra for rolling

1 egg

1 teaspoon vanilla extract

½ cup dark molasses

MIX

1. Sift the flour, baking soda, salt, and spices into a bowl and set it aside.

2. Cream the butter and sugars on medium speed for several minutes until light and fluffy. Add the egg and vanilla and mix until combined. Add the molasses and mix until combined.

3. Add the flour mixture in thirds and mix on low just until incorporated.

4. Cover the dough and refrigerate for 15 to 20 minutes.

BAKE

5. Line several cookie sheets with parchment paper or silicone mats. Roll 1½-inch balls of dough in the extra sugar. Place the cookies on the baking sheets about 2 inches apart. Bake

CONTINUED

SPICY

for 9 to 11 minutes, rotating the halfway through baking. (For crispy cookies, leave them in for another minute or two.) Cool the sheets on wire racks for about 5 minutes before transferring cookies directly onto racks to cool.

ADD FROSTING

These cookies are chewy and delicious on their own, but it never hurts to spread on a little frosting.

Iced Molasses Spice Cookies
Slather on a thin layer of Creamy Vanilla Frosting (page 28) or decorate with store-bought white royal icing.

NOTES:

Salt-and-Pepper Cookies

It might be cheating to call these savory little nibbles cookies, but once you bite into one, all rules go out the door. They're made in a food processor (hello, simple), and I swear the scent will nearly floor you when you open the oven for the first time. Instant mouth watering. The result is beyond what you're imagining: as flaky and buttery as the bottom of a fresh-baked biscuit, with little bursts of coarse salt that dissolve on your tongue. Serve a few on the side of a bowl of chili or hot soup.

PREHEAT OVEN TO 300°F

MAKES: 2½ DOZEN COOKIES

1½ cups all-purpose flour

½ cup cold, unsalted butter, cut into small pieces

1 teaspoon kosher salt, plus more for topping

1¼ teaspoons cracked black pepper, plus more for topping

1 teaspoon lemon zest

1 egg

 MIX

1. Whir the flour and butter together in a food processor until they form fine crumbs. Add the salt, cracked pepper, and lemon zest and zap again to combine.

2. Add the egg and blend until the dough starts to come together.

3. Roll out the dough to about ¼-inch thick on a lightly floured surface. Using a round cookie cutter or biscuit cutter to a size of your liking (don't go any bigger than 1¾ inches around), cut out the coins and place them on sheets about 1½ inches apart.

 tip

You can go as thin as $1/8$ inch, but I prefer them thicker and softer.

 BAKE

4. Brush the cookies with a little egg white and sprinkle the cracked peppercorns and

 CONTINUED

SPICY

Salt-and-Pepper Cookies, cont'd...

salt on top. Go easy on the extra! It's mostly for decoration—the cookies are plenty flavorful without it.

5. Bake for 15 to 18 minutes, until the cookies start to take on a lovely golden color. Let cool.

MORE TO TRY

White Pepper Cookies
Substitute cracked white pepper for the black pepper.

Opt for white pepper if you prefer a milder taste. White peppercorns are less potent because they've had their skins removed.

NOTES:

Snickerdoodles

They're a little sweet, a little spicy, and so easy to make. (The dough is similar to sugar cookie dough, but rolled in cinnamon-sugar before baking.) Plus, aren't they fun to pronounce?

PREHEAT OVEN TO 350°F

MAKES:
2 DOZEN COOKIES

1⅓ cups all-purpose flour
½ teaspoon cream of tartar
½ teaspoon baking soda
⅛ teaspoon salt
½ cup unsalted butter, at room temperature
½ cup plus 2 tablespoons sugar
2 tablespoons light brown sugar
1 egg
1 teaspoon vanilla extract

For rolling:
¼ cup sugar
4 teaspoons cinnamon

 MIX

1. Grease several cookie sheets or line them with parchment paper. Set aside. Next sift the flour, cream of tartar, baking soda, and salt into a bowl and set it aside as well.

2. Cream the butter and both sugars on medium speed for several minutes until they're light and fluffy. Add the egg and vanilla and mix to combine.

3. Add the flour mixture in two batches, making sure the first half is incorporated before adding the second. Stop when the second batch is fully combined.

BAKE 4. Stir together cinnamon and sugar in a bowl. Roll 1-inch balls of dough into the mixture. Place them on the cookie sheets about

CONTINUED

Snickerdoodles, cont'd...

2 inches apart, or slightly more if you think you've had a heavy hand. Flatten the balls of dough slightly with the palm of your hand.

5. Bake the cookies 9 to 10 minutes, if you like them chewy, or 12 to 13 minutes, if you prefer crispy. Cool the sheets on wire racks for a few minutes, then transfer the cookies directly onto the racks to let them finish cooling.

MORE TO TRY

How could Snickerdoodles possibly get any more delicious? Peanut butter.

Peanut Butter Cup–doodles
Chop or smash a few pieces of miniature peanut butter cups into each cookie before rolling in the cinnamon sugar.

Peanut Butter Chip–doodles
Mix peanut butter chips into the batter before forming the dough into balls.

Peanut Butter Sandwich–doodles
Mash together 3 tablespoons unsalted butter (at room temperature), 1/4 cup smooth peanut butter (not natural), 2/3 cup confectioners' sugar, and 1/4 teaspoon salt. Spread on the bottom side of one cooled cookie and top with another.

NOTES:

NOTES:

SPICY

NUTTY & SEEDY

129
ALMOND BISCOTTI

135
PEANUT
BUTTER
COOKIES

POPPY SEED SQUARES

145

148
SESAME CRISPS

133
CARAMEL
NUT BARS

137
PECAN SANDIES

140
PIGNOLI
COOKIES

131
ALMOND CRESCENTS

143
PISTACHIO BUTTER COOKIES

Almond Biscotti

I'm not really a lingerer at the table. For a little lady, I take serious bites (and I like second helpings while they're still warm, please). But at the oven, things are different. This biscotti recipe is for the slow Sunday cook in all of us. The name means "twice baked," and they are, so there's no rushing to the finish line. This recipe can be varied in any number of ways—you can change up the nuts, add dried fruit, replace the almond extract with citrus zest, the list goes on and on. But start with the original first. I swear, you'll want to make a batch every week.

PREHEAT OVEN TO 350°F

MAKES: 3 DOZEN COOKIES

1¾ cups all-purpose flour

¼ cup cornmeal

1 cup sugar

1 teaspoon baking soda

½ teaspoon salt

2 eggs

1 teaspoon vanilla extract*

4 tablespoons unsalted butter, melted

1 cup almonds, coarsely chopped

✱ Or almond extract.

 MIX

1. Beat together the flour, cornmeal, sugar, baking soda, and salt. Add the eggs, working them in one at a time until fully incorporated.

2. Add the vanilla and butter, mixing well until the dough begins to form. It will not come together completely. Add the almonds and stir to evenly distribute.

 BAKE

3. Turn out the dough onto a cookie sheet with lightly floured hands. Divide it in half and shape it into two logs, each about 1½ inch thick and 2 inches wide.

 tip

The mixture will look dry and crumbly.

CONTINUED

Almond Biscotti, cont'd...

4. Bake the biscotti for 20 minutes (this is the first of 2 times you'll be baking them), rotating the sheet halfway through baking. Take it out and let the logs rest on the sheet for 20 minutes. They'll still be slightly spongy to the touch, kind of like dense bread. Lower the oven temp to 250°F.

Slice biscotti in one quick motion— no sawing.

5. After 20 minutes, transfer the logs to a cutting board. Cut them into ½-inch slices using a serrated knife. Finally, move the slices (cut side up for any ends) back to one sheet and bake for 40 minutes more. The biscotti will still be slightly soft while warm but will harden fully once they've cooled.

MORE TO TRY

Add flavors, chocolate, fruit or nut mix-ins—or dip baked biscotti in melted chocolate.

Lemony Biscotti
Add the zest of 1 lemon when you add the vanilla.

Chocolate-Dipped Biscotti
Dip either the flat side of the biscotti or one of the pointy tips into melted chocolate, following the directions for dipping on page 147. Use melted bittersweet or semisweet chocolate.

directions for dipping on page 147.

NOTES:

NUTTY+SEEDY

Almond Crescents
DUSTED WITH SUGAR

When these crumbly almond cookies melt in your mouth, the toasty, nutty bits are left behind. The cookies taste even better rolled in granulated sugar.

PREHEAT OVEN TO 350°F

MAKES:
2 DOZEN COOKIES

½ cup ground almonds

½ cup powdered sugar

½ cup unsalted butter, at room temperature

1½ teaspoons vanilla extract

1 teaspoon almond extract

1 cup all-purpose flour

1/8 teaspoon salt

½ cup sugar, for coating

MIX

1. Sift the ground almonds and powdered sugar into a bowl and set it aside.

2. Beat butter on medium speed for several minutes until smooth. Add in the almond mixture and mix until combined. Add the vanilla and almond extracts and mix until combined. Add the flour and salt and mix on low just until combined and the dough starts to take shape.

BAKE

3. Turn the dough out onto a piece of plastic wrap, wrap tightly, and chill for about 20 minutes to firm up slightly.

4. Line several cookie sheets with parchment paper or silicone baking mats. Form the dough into 1-inch balls. Roll them into little logs between your fingers and curve the ends to make a crescent shape. Place on cookie sheets about 1½ inches apart.

CONTINUED

NUTTY+SEEDY

Almond Crescents, cont'd...

5. Bake for 8 to 10 minutes, rotating the sheets halfway through baking.

6. The edges of the cookies should turn light brown, but the tops should not get too dark. Cool sheets on wire racks for a few minutes. While the crescents are still hanging onto their last bit of warmth, roll them in the vanilla sugar to coat. Let them finish cooling on wire racks.

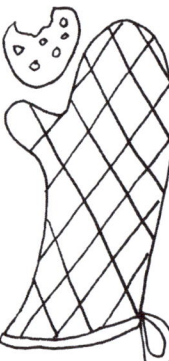

NOTES:

MORE TO TRY

Snowy Almond Crescents
Roll the cookies in powdered sugar after they've mostly cooled.

Nutty Crescents
Change up the nuts! Use pecans, walnuts, hazelnuts, or Brazil nuts in place of almonds and omit the almond extract.

Vanilla Almond Crescents
Roll the cookies in vanilla sugar (instead of regular) while they're still warm from the oven Vanilla sugar can be store-bought or homemade with the easy recipe on page 30.

NUTTY+SEEDY

Caramel Nut Bars
WITH A BUTTERY SHORTBREAD CRUST

If you've ever been intimidated by making homemade caramel, I have a secret for you: It's just melting sugar in a saucepan! Granted, caramelized sugar can get extremely hot and you should exercise good caution while working with it, but making it merely involves a few swirls of the wrist and a little temperature taking. Once you taste it— so salty, so luxurious—on these thick and chewy caramel nut bars, you'll doubly applaud yourself for the courage.

PREHEAT OVEN TO 350°F

MAKES:
12 SQUARES

1½ cups mixed nuts*

For the crust:

1½ cups all-purpose flour
¼ cup plus 2 tablespoons sugar
   pinch salt
¾ cup cold unsalted butter, cut into pieces

For the topping:

1½ cups sugar
 1 teaspoon coarse salt
½ teaspoon lemon juice
¼ cup plus 2 tablespoons heavy cream

✳ Such as cashews, peanuts, hazelnuts, or macadamia.

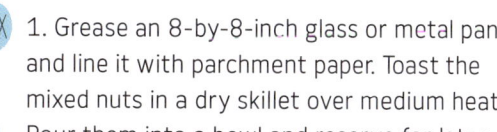

MIX

1. Grease an 8-by-8-inch glass or metal pan and line it with parchment paper. Toast the mixed nuts in a dry skillet over medium heat. Pour them into a bowl and reserve for later.

2. In the meantime, make the crust. Combine the ingredients in a food processor or mixer on low speed until a coarse meal is formed. Pour out the crumby dough into the prepared pan and gently press it into the bottom in an even layer. Bake for 20 minutes, until it is golden, firm, and dry. Let cool.

BAKE

3. Get started on making the topping. Pour the sugar into a heavy-bottomed saucepan and pour in the coarse salt and lemon juice. Stir in ¾ cup water and cook over high heat until the sugar melts and begins to darken. This

tip

Choose one that's at least medium to large in size.

CONTINUED

NUTTY+SEEDY

Caramel Nut Bars, cont'd...

should take about 5 minutes. When you see the color change, lower the heat to medium and keep cooking, swirling the pan so it cooks and colors evenly, until the sugar is completely melted and the caramel is amber in color and registers 300°F on a candy thermometer (or what the pros call hard-crack stage).

4. With a wooden spoon, slowly pour the cream into the pan—it will splatter, but just stand back and keep pouring bravely in a steady stream while stirring constantly. Take the caramel off the heat, add a tablespoon of butter, and let it cool for 15 minutes.

5. Sprinkle the nuts into the cooled caramel and stir them around. Pour and spread the mixture over the crust and bake the whole thing again so the caramel can firm up, about 10 minutes. Let cool completely before cutting into squares.

tip To test the consistency of your caramel while it cooks, carefully drop a spoonful into a bowl of icy water. The consistency it takes on will be similar to what it feels like in the finished bars.

MORE TO TRY

Pine Nut Bars
Substitute the mixed nuts for lightly toasted pine nuts.

NOTES:

Peanut Butter Cookies

This cookie has gone mainstream for a reason: It's salty and sweet and out of this world when served with a tall glass of cold milk—total comfort food. This version has a surprisingly light, crumbly texture.

PREHEAT OVEN TO 375°F

MAKES:
3 DOZEN COOKIES

½ cup unsalted butter,
        at room temperature
½ cup light brown sugar
½ cup sugar
1 egg
½ teaspoon vanilla extract
1 cup creamy peanut butter*
1¼ cups all-purpose flour
½ teaspoon baking soda
½ teaspoon salt
   Granulated sugar for
        sprinkling

✷ Or chunky, if you prefer it.
   But avoid natural peanut
   butters, (unless you want to
   experiment) as they'll yield
   different results.

MIX

1. Cream the butter and sugars for a minute or two until they look light and fluffy. Add the egg and vanilla and continue to mix until combined.

2. Add the peanut butter—get every last drop with a spatula—and mix until completely combined. The mixture will start to look silky and smell peanuty.

3. Sift the flour with the baking soda and salt. Add the flour mixture to the butter mixture half at a time and mix on low speed just until combined. Now you're in business.

4. Drop tablespoon-sized balls of dough onto lightly greased or parchment-paper-lined cookie sheets, leaving about 3 inches between for them to grow. Using a fork, press down on each ball of dough to flatten and create a

tip

Try not to go much larger; the dough expands.

CONTINUED

Peanut Butter Cookies, cont'd...

cross-hatch pattern. Sprinkle the tops with a lot of granulated sugar.

 5. Bake for 9 to 11 minutes, until they're just starting to have golden hints around the edges. Take them out while they still look a little soft for a light, crumby cookie. Transfer the cookies onto wire racks to cool.

MORE TO TRY

Double Peanut Butter Sandwiches
Press cookies extra thin with your fork before baking. Once fully cooled, fill with Peanut Butter Filling (recipe on page 50).

Peanut Butter and Jelly Cookies
Skip the granulated sugar and the cross-hatching. When the cookies first come out of the oven, use the handle of a wooden spoon to gently make a hole in the center of each. Drop about 1 teaspoon (or a little less) of jam into the hole. Wait about 5 minutes and then transfer the cookies to a wire rack with a spatula to finish cooling.

Peanut Butter Blossoms
Skip the cross-hatching. Just before baking, press a chocolate kiss into the center of each cookie.

NOTES:

NUTTY+SEEDY

Pecan Sandies
WITH BEAUTIFUL TOASTED PECANS

Some baked goods—like sliced bagels, fresh English muffins, and thin-crust pizza—just beg to be toasted. Don't fight it! Bring out the flavor in this shortbread-reminiscent dough by toasting all the nuts (not just the whole ones for garnishing) in a dry skillet before mixing them into the batter. Then bake the cookies until the edges take on a golden-brown tone. They'll simply fall apart in your mouth.

PREHEAT OVEN TO 325°F

MAKES:
2½ DOZEN COOKIES

1½ cups pecans, dry-toasted in a skillet

⅓ cup powdered sugar

⅔ cup light brown sugar

1½ cups all-purpose flour, plus 1 to 2 tablespoons for dusting

½ teaspoon coarse salt

¾ cup plus 2 tablespoons cold unsalted butter,* cut into 1-inch cubes

1 egg

1 teaspoon vanilla extract

About 30 pecan halves for decorating

Sugar for dusting

* What goes better with toastiness than butter? Splurge on a good-quality one to ensure a rich and creamy flavor, and a perfect crumbly texture.

MIX

1. In a food processor, finely grind the pecans with the sugars.

2. Add the flour and salt and buzz again until combined. Add the butter and process until the mixture starts to look sort of pebbly, like coarse crumbs. Then you can add the egg and vanilla. Keep processing until the dough comes together.

3. Lightly dust a clean surface with the remaining flour and turn out the dough on top. Form the dough into a ball and then flatten it into a disk, working in some of the flour from the table, as needed. Wrap in plastic wrap and place in the freezer for about 30 minutes or in the refrigerator for at least 1 hour. The dough should be slightly firm so you can roll it with a rolling pin.

CONTINUED

Pecan Sandies, cont'd...

BAKE

4. Roll to about ¼-inch thick, sprinkling the surface and the rolling pin with flour it if starts to stick. Cut out cookies from the chilled dough with a 2-inch cookie cutter. Space them about an inch apart on parchment-paper-lined baking sheets.

5. Place one of the beautiful toasted pecan halves in the center of each cookie and dust with a light sprinkling of sugar. Bake 18 to 20 minutes, or until the cookies are a lovely sandy color, rotating the sheets halfway through baking. Cool the cookies completely before storing them in airtight containers or vintage tins.

tip

These cookies store best flat. Lay them on pieces of parchment paper in a cookie tin, plastic storage container, or cardboard bakery box.

MORE TO TRY

Snowy Sandies

Skip dusting the cookies with granulated sugar. Instead, sift powdered sugar over the tops of the sandies once they've completely cooked.

NOTES:

Pignoli Cookies

They might look delicate, but these yummy pine nut cookies are entirely forgiving to work with. A careless roll around the nut bowl and they come out beautiful every time.

PREHEAT OVEN TO 300°F

MAKES:
2½ DOZEN COOKIES

½ cup sugar

½ cup powdered sugar

¼ cup all-purpose flour

$^1/_8$ teaspoon salt

¾ cup (8 oz) almond paste at room temperature

2 egg whites

1 cup pine nuts

MIX

1. Sift the sugars, flour, and salt into a bowl and set it aside.

2. Beat the almond paste on low speed for several minutes until it is broken up into small pea-sized pieces. Give the egg whites a quick whisk, then add half to the bowl and continue mixing.

3. Add the flour mixture and beat until well combined. There might be some small pieces of almond paste that will not smooth out, but this won't affect the cookies. Add the remaining egg white and continue mixing until well combined. Cover the dough in plastic wrap and refrigerate for 1 hour.

BAKE

4. Line several cookie sheets with parchment paper. Scoop out teaspoonfuls of dough and roll them into neat balls, then roll the balls in the pine nuts.

5. Place them on baking sheets at least 2 inches apart. Bake 18 minutes, or until light golden brown, rotating the sheets halfway through baking. Cool for 15 minutes, then carefully peel the cookies off the parchment paper.

Metal tins block out moisture better than cardboard or plastic storage containers. Consider packing cookies in pretty vintage boxes tied with baker's twine or loaf pans layered with parchment paper.

MAKE SANDWICH COOKIES

Double up pignoli with a generous spread of creamy homemade chocolate ganache.*

Ganache

Melt 4 ounces of chopped semisweet chocolate over a double boiler and stir in 2 tablespoons of heavy cream. Let cool and stiffen slightly and then spread between cookies with an offset spatula.

✳ Equally delicious sandwiched between other cookies.

NOTES:

Pistachio Butter Cookies

Don't tell the other cookies in this book, but these green beauties may be my hands-down favorite. The recipe practically invented itself on a wintry Sunday morning in my kitchen. Once I had ground the pistachios into a gorgeous olive-oily paste, a dose of the darkest brown sugar seemed like the only appropriate contrast. Flooded with a tongue-happying salty-nutty flavor and plenty of baked-in sugary crystals, the chewy result is borderline indescribable. Okay, I'm stopping now.

PREHEAT OVEN TO 350°F

MAKES: 2½ DOZEN COOKIES

MIX

1 cup raw unsalted pistachios
2 tablespoons olive or pistachio oil
½ cup unsalted butter, softened
¾ cup sugar
½ cup firmly packed brown sugar
1 large egg, at room temperature
½ teaspoon vanilla extract
1¼ cups all-purpose flour
¾ teaspoon baking soda
½ teaspoon baking powder
½ teaspoon kosher salt
Sugar, for rolling (optional)

1. Make the luscious pistachio butter: Grind the pistachios in the food processor until a fine meal forms. Then slowly drizzle in the oil with the motor running until it becomes a paste. It won't be completely smooth. That's okay.

2. Beat the pistachio butter and the regular butter together until they look smooth, then add both sugars and continue beating until fluffy. Add the egg and mix to incorporate, then pour in the vanilla and mix again.

3. Stir together the flour, baking soda, baking powder, and salt in a bowl.

4. Add it into the pistachio mixture a third at a time, pausing to let each batch incorporate before adding the next.

CONTINUED

NUTTY+SEEDY

Pistachio Butter Cookies, cont'd...

BAKE

5. Scoop out tablespoon-sized balls onto parchment-paper-lined cookie sheets at least 2 inches apart. Bake for 9 to 11 minutes, just until you start to see hints of golden. The cookies will look puffy when you first take them out, but they'll flatten and get nice and craggly as they cool.

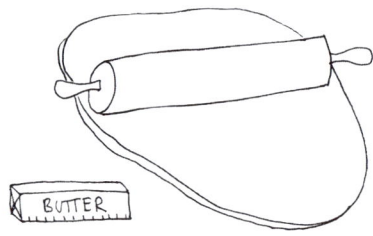

SUPERSIZE THEM

This cookie's dough is the type that's perfect if you like to make big chewy cookies the size of your head.

Giant Pistachio Cookies
Form dough into large balls—about 2 full teaspoons each—and bake leaving 2 to 3 inches between cookies.

NOTES:

Poppy Seed Squares
WITH CHOCOLATE TIPS

Some people might think poppy seeds aren't the sexiest of cookie mix-ins. These crispy, poppy-flecked cookies beg to differ. The little blue-gray beads add both a nutty flavor and a crunchy texture, bringing a savory depth to this shortbread-style dough. Balance it all out with a healthy dunk into sweet melted chocolate.

PREHEAT OVEN TO 275°F

MAKES:
3 DOZEN COOKIES

1 cup unsalted butter, at room temperature
2 cups all-purpose flour
5 tablespoons rice flour
1/3 cup sugar
1 tablespoon poppy seeds
Pinch salt

For dipping:
12 ounces (about 1 bar) chocolate
1/4 cup unsalted butter

MIX

1. Beat the butter until very light and creamy. Sift the flour into a separate bowl, then add it to the butter and continue to mix until it looks crumby.

2. Add the rice flour, sugar, poppy seeds, and a pinch of salt. Mix until all is blended thoroughly. The mixture will still look like loose crumbs.

3. Use the warmth of your hand to form the dough into a ball. Divide it in half and roll out the first half on a floured surface to 1/2-inch thick. Cut the dough into squares or rectangles, then scoop up the scraps and add them to the remaining dough. Roll out the remaining dough and cut it into more squares.

CONTINUED

Poppy Seed Squares, cont'd...

 BAKE

4. Lightly butter and flour a cookie sheet and place the cookies on the sheet. They can be pretty close together. Bake for 30 to 35 minutes, until they just start to take on a brown tinge. Remove, let cool for a few minutes, then transfer to a rack to finish cooling.

5. Break up the chocolate into a bowl and set it over a small pot of simmering water. Add the butter and stir until it's finally melted and looks glossy and smooth. Remove from heat and let cool slightly.

6. One by one dunk cookies in chocolate, pulling away to let the excess drop off. Lay them on parchment-lined sheets (or wire racks with parchment under them) to set.

 **tip** Make sure the bowl doesn't touch the water to avoid burning the chocolate.

VARIATIONS

Add (More) Seeds
Lightly sprinkle sesame seeds onto the chocolate before it hardens.

Top with Nuts
Dunk each chocolate-coated cookie end into a bowl of chopped, toasted almonds before laying it to dry.

NOTES:

Sesame Crisps
WITH TOASTED SEEDS

Anytime I think of these cookies, my mouth puckers a little bit—in a good way. The batter is made with almost equal quantities dark brown sugar and fragrant sesame seeds, and it comes together in a tart-sweet, nutty caramel flavor in your mouth. Whether I owe it to that or to the fact these can be made in 10 minutes with no mixer, these are my go-to for a last-possible-second sugar fix.

PREHEAT OVEN TO 375°F

MAKES:
3 DOZEN COOKIES

1   cup sesame seeds
1   cup all-purpose flour
¼   teaspoon baking soda
¼   teaspoon salt
1½ cups dark brown sugar
¾   cup unsalted butter, melted
1   egg
1   teaspoon vanilla extract

 MIX

1. Spread the sesame seeds in as even a layer as possible in a large nonstick skillet. Toast them over medium-low heat for 6 to 8 minutes, stirring occasionally, until lightly browned and fragrant. Remove from the heat and pour into a large bowl. Add the flour, baking soda, and salt and set aside.

2. In a separate bowl, combine the sugar, melted butter, egg, and vanilla and stir until fully combined. Slowly add the flour mixture and stir to incorporate.

BAKE

3. Pipe the batter with a bag, or drop it by teaspoonfuls, onto parchment-paper-lined cookie sheets about 2 inches apart. Try to go no bigger than an inch in diameter.

4. Bake the cookies for 6 to 8 minutes, or until browned around the edges, rotating the sheets halfway through baking. Let them cool on the sheet for a minute or two before lifting them to a wire rack.

MAKE 'EM DUNKABLE

These savory-sweet treats are the perfect pick-me-up snack.

Coffee-break Cookies

For a cookie that's better suited for coffee dunking, pipe the batter in 2-inch lines down the parchment paper to make sesame bars instead.

NOTES:

Cookiepedia Index

Cookiepedia Index, cont'd...

01 14